Success Secrets from Silicon Valley

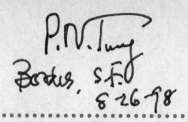

SUCCESS SECRETS

FROM

SILICON VALLEY

How to Make Your Teams More Effective

(No Matter What Business You're In)

GEOFFREY JAMES

TIMES BUSINESS

RANDOM HOUSE

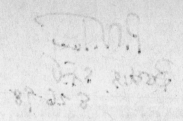

This work was originally published in hardcover and in different form as *Business Wisdom of the Electronic Elite* in 1996 by Times Books, a division of Random House, Inc.

James, Geoffrey
    Success secrets from Silicon Valley : how to make your teams more effective (no matter what business you're in) / Geoffrey James.— 1st ed.
        p.   cm.
    Rev. ed. of: Business wisdom of the electronic elite. 1st ed. ©1996.
    Includes index.
    ISBN 0-8129-2976-4 (pbk. : alk. paper)
    1. High technology industries—Management.   2. Corporate culture.
3. Organizational effectiveness.   4. Office practice—Automation.
5. Leadership.   I. James, Geoffrey, 1953–   Business wisdom of the electronic elite.   II. Title.
HD62.37.J349   1998
820'.0068—dc21   97-41732

Random House website address: www.randomhouse.com

Printed in the United States of America on acid free paper

9 8 7 6 5 4 3 2

First Revised Paperback Edition

For Rebecca

"The Top 50 Companies,
Leigh Weimer's Guide to
Silicon Valley" 1993

"No Top 30 Companies,"
Leigh Weimers Guide to
Silicon Valley 1995

Contents

Contents

Key No. 3: Management
Is Service, Not Control

Key No. 4: Employees
Are Peers, Not Children

Contents

Key No. 5: Motivate with Vision, Not Fear

Key No. 6: Change Is Growth, Not Pain

Key No. 7: Computers Are Servants, Not Masters

Contents

THE NEW
CORPORATE CULTURE

Do you remember the year 1984? That was the year that President Reagan defeated Mondale in the U.S. presidential election. It was the year that *Terms of Endearment* won an academy award and the film *Amadeus* was making Mozart into a household word. Michael Jackson's *Thriller* album won eight Grammy awards after selling a whopping 37 million copies. And it was the year that the space shuttle Discovery made its first, historic flight.

But the space shuttle wasn't the only thing flying high in 1984. It was a great year for a company with the acronym, IBM. In 1984, IBM completely dominated the computer industry—the fastest growing and most profitable industry on the planet. IBM had fanatically loyal customers, customers who used to say, with pride in their voices: "Nobody ever gets fired for buying IBM." IBM had an enormous war chest—more than enough money to send an entire corporate army to capture any market. IBM had legendary management—with probably more MBAs per capita than any other company. IBM had extraordinary brand name equity, the kind of market recognition that consistently drove IBM to the top of *Fortune* magazine's poll of the most highly respected companies. And to top it all off, IBM had just invented what was destined to become the most popular computer product in the world—the famous IBM personal computer.

The year 1984 was also the year in which a certain 18-year-old entered college for the first time—an 18-year-old who would soon threaten the market dominance of industrial giant IBM. I'd like you to remember what it was like being a college freshman for a moment. I live close to Boston, which is a big college town, and whenever I go downtown, I see many college students. Do you know how you can tell the freshmen from the rest of the students? The freshmen are the ones wearing only one nose ring. Of course, nose rings weren't the fashion back in 1984, but as I'm talking about this particular college freshman, I'd like you to imagine somebody who, if he were in college today, might just be thinking of getting his nose pierced. This idea helps put this story into perspective.

Like most college freshmen, the biggest worry for this young man was what to do on Saturday night. He must have ended up with spare time on his hands, because he decided to start his own business. Thirteen years later, that company—Dell Computer—sells as many personal computers as IBM. It's grown to employ some 8,000 people, while IBM has had to downsize half of its employees. More importantly, most industry analysts consider Dell Computer to be the pace-setter in the PC industry, due to the company's constant innovations in all areas of the business, from design to manufacturing to distribution.

The story of Michael Dell and the rise of Dell Computer is the stuff of legends, but sometimes we don't think about how miraculous the legend truly is. Consider: IBM had everything going for it: gigantic revenues, loyal customers, enormous capital, great management, an incredible image, and the hottest product on the market. Michael Dell had *no* revenues, *no* customers, *no* capital, *no* experience, *no* market image, and *no* product to call his own. And still Dell won.

With this in mind, I want you to ask yourself two questions:

1. *What was it that allowed some wet-behind-the-ears college kid to grow a wildly successful business in the face of entrenched competition from the most powerful corporation in the entire world?*
2. *How successful could your career and your organization become if you could tap into whatever it was that made Michael Dell and Dell Computer so wildly successful?*

These questions are important because the management techniques that Michael Dell used to grow his business can be applied to nearly any business. They're already working inside corporations from coast to coast and overseas as well. They represent a major change in the way that organizations are managed and the way that teams are built. I call them the *Success Secrets from Silicon Valley.*

Silicon Valley, a Pacific coastal valley on the western shores of the San Francisco bay, has for the past twenty years been the homeland of the computer industry. It contains the headquarters of many of the most famous high-tech companies in the world: Hewlett-Packard, Apple Computer, Silicon Graphics, Oracle, and Intel, just to name a few. Silicon Valley is to high-tech industry what Hollywood is to the entertainment industry. While there are other clusters of high-tech businesses in the U.S. and elsewhere, much of the "action" in the computer industry takes place there.

Silicon Valley is also the birthplace of a new kind of business culture—a way of creating, building, and managing corporations that's very different from the traditional way that companies were run in the past.

This book describes that culture, which has since spread from its roots in Silicon Valley into companies like Microsoft, Dell Computer, Acer, and Compaq—all of which are headquartered far from Silicon Valley but which remain part of the same cultural milieu.

Traditional Business Culture Says:	Silicon Valley Culture Says:
Bigger is better, biggest is best.	Stay lean, run hard, move quick.
Markets are territory to be conquered.	Treat customers like business partners.
Destroy the competition and leave no wounded.	Compete today and cooperate tomorrow.
Hide your mistakes from the other sharks.	Let the organization learn from your mistakes.
Lecture employees on company loyalty.	Throw a company party in the parking lot.
Always keep the bastards guessing.	Always explain why you've made a decision.
You can't trust people, especially employees.	Let people alone and they'll do the right thing.
Success is having a big staff and a big budget.	Success is feeling good about what you do.

Many aspects of the way business is conducted in Silicon Valley have also disseminated into the rest of the business world. For example:

- *First Name Informality.* The first company to start breaking down the stultifying formality between management and workers was Hewlett-Packard, which instituted "first names" as a corporate policy in 1939. Today, calling managers and executives by their first names is becoming common even in highly traditional firms.
- *Casual Dress.* Casual dress for professionals started inside companies like Microsoft. As time goes on, more companies are shedding their dress codes and letting people wear what's comfortable and appropriate.
- *Flextime.* High-tech firms were among the first to allow employees to work irregular hours, allowing them greater flexibility to manage the rest of their lives. While many traditional corporations are resisting the change, flextime and working at home is becoming increasingly common.
- *Employee Ownership.* High-tech firms pioneered the use of employee equity to create employee loyalty, even in markets where job security was impossible. Today, most corporations have some form of stock ownership, and some (like Starbucks Coffee) extend such plans even to part-timers.

There's a reason that the business culture of Silicon Valley is slipping into the boardrooms and backrooms of nearly every industry. The reason: It works! This new way of doing business creates organizations and teams that are flexible and powerful, adaptable yet determined, well able to overcome companies that cling to the old rules of doing business.

However, to understand why and how this the Silicon Valley culture works, we need return to the years before the term "Silicon Valley" had ever been coined.

A Little History

The 1970s were glory years for the computer industry, full of energy and optimism. The invention of the integrated circuit made it possible to create computers that were faster and more powerful than ever before. Demand for computers was high, and profit margins were even higher. Career advancement was automatic. Anyone lucky enough to be employed by a computer vendor was guaranteed a bright future.

The traditional computer vendors were dominated by IBM, which made more money each year than all its competitors combined. IBM's competition was a set of mainframe vendors that had been around as long as IBM itself. These were the so-called BUNCH, an acronym that stood for Boroughs, Univac, NCR, Control Data, and Honeywell. In addition to the BUNCH, a group of vendors sold the smaller mainframes called minicomputers; these vendors included Digital, Data General, Prime, Wang, and a host of others.

Until the early 1980s, it looked as though the computer industry's glory years would continue forever. Profits were up. The traditional mainframe and minicomputer vendors seemed to just keep on growing. Few people inside the computer industry guessed that in another five years or so, all of it would be a memory.

What changed the computer industry was the microprocessor. The microprocessor was a "computer on a chip" that made it vastly less expensive to provide computing power to individual workers. This radical drop in the price of computer power changed the way that computers were manufactured, distributed, purchased, and used. In the 1970s, computers were so big and so complicated that customers were forced to buy from a single vendor who sold the entire unit as a big-ticket item. These transactions involved so much money and effort that the computer vendor and the customer needed a very close relationship. Some IBM salespeople, for example, even had their offices at their customer's establishment.

The microprocessor changed all this. The old minicomputers and mainframes were cumbersome, complex devices. The microprocessor made it possible to put the power of a mainframe on everyone's desktop. Rapid advances in technology made computers so cheap that the computer power that would have cost $1 million in 1970 had dropped to about $100 by 1995. To put this into perspective, if computers were automobiles, you could buy the transportation equivalent of a 1970 Toyota for about a dollar today.

The microprocessor also meant that computers could be sold off the shelf, like stereo systems. It was no longer necessary, or economical, to have high-priced salespeople at customer sites. For many applications, a customer could buy a computer at a local storefront computer store. Whereas in the past purchasing a computer had been a major corporate decision requiring multiple signatures, now just about anybody could afford to buy a personal computer. Line managers with microscopic budgets could afford as much computer power as the corporate heavies who ran the giant mainframes. This created an explosion of buying activity, as professionals around the world began to demand—and receive—control over their own computing resources.

The microprocessor also fueled an amazing burst of creativity in the field of software. Programmers began designing new products that could take advantage of this new source of inexpensive computing power. Excellent word processing, spreadsheet, and database programs flooded the market.

The microprocessor and the ensuing software revolution created an enormous demand for computer products. And where there's demand, there's money to be made. Somebody was going to reap the profits. Who better than the traditional computer companies who had been building and manufacturing similar products for almost 20 years?

Think about it! The traditional minicomputer and mainframe vendors had everything going for them. They had plenty of cash, more than enough to launch new methods of manufacturing and marketing. The traditional vendors also had great technology. After all, IBM actually invented the standard personal computer that's so popular today. Similarly, Digital, the minicomputer vendor, had software in the 1970s—such as electronic mail and electronic conferencing—that's only now becoming common on personal computers and networks. Even more important, the traditional vendors had reputations for being very well run. Digital's founder Ken Olsen was, as late as 1988, being touted in the business press as the "ultimate entrepreneur." Big war chests, great technology, legendary management—a recipe for certain success, you'd think. But it didn't work out that way.

By 1995, the BUNCH had disappeared in a flurry of mergers and downsizings. Univac and Boroughs had merged and shrunk beyond recognition. Honeywell's computer division had emigrated to France, only staying alive as the result of government charity. NCR had vanished into AT&T only to reappear in a blaze of layoffs. Control Data had almost completely disappeared.

The minicomputer vendors fared little better. Wang declared bankruptcy. Prime and Data General shriveled into nonentities. Digital, once the darling of Wall Street, managed to lose $1.75 billion in a single quarter, an incredible amount considering that Digital's earnings peaked at $1.3 billion a year in

1988. Of the ten or so minicomputer vendors that were profitable in 1980, only Hewlett-Packard remained a major force in the industry 15 years later, having successfully diversified into personal computer printers and engineering workstations.

Of the traditional mainframe vendors, only IBM is reasonably intact. However, it was forced to lay off nearly half of its 400,000-plus workforce, and still faces many challenges. IBM has watched its lead in personal computers shrink year after year and has been upstart competitors eat away at its market share. While IBM is financially strong at the time of this writing, it's unclear whether this can remain the case unless the company recaptures some of its lost industry leadership.

Despite the troubles of the traditional computer vendors, the computer industry as a whole has continued to grow. This growth, however, has been captured by an entirely new set of companies. Some of these upstarts are software companies, such as Microsoft (operating systems) and Oracle (databases). Some, including Compaq and Dell, make personal computers; and others, like Sun and Silicon Graphics, make high-priced specialty workstation systems. While a number of the traditional computer vendors are still around in watered-down, stripped-to-the-bone incarnations, it's clear to people both inside and outside the computer industry that a major transformation has taken place.

The irony here is that according to conventional business wisdom, the large, established vendors should have had no problem making the transition to the new products. By all rights, they should easily have been able to overpower the upstarts. An entire industry, consisting of some of the most respected companies in the world, was driven into obscurity and financial ruin by raggle-taggle upstarts seemingly coming from out of nowhere.

And the same thing could happen—and may already be happening—in your industry as well. Because the driving force behind the transformation of the high-tech world—massive computerization—is becoming common inside every industry today. The same internal forces that made it possible for Dell and Microsoft to overtake IBM and Digital are now beginning to work their weird magic in your own company and among your competitors as well. For you and your company, this can be either a disaster or an incredible opportunity.

The Changing World of Business

It's stating the obvious to point out that computers have changed the world. The effect of computers on nearly every aspect of our daily lives is so pervasive and so complete that it's difficult to envision the modern world without them. Our economic systems are completely dependent on computers to measure, transmit, and verify financial transactions. The global telecommunications network that brings information from around the world to our living rooms and boardrooms is a result of this vast technological explosion. Computers are everywhere, embedded in our automobiles, televisions, and microwave ovens. The personal computer has become nearly as common as the telephone on the desks of American workers.

The computerization of the business world has had an enormous effect on corporations, and as a result, many of the most respected corporations of the past are experiencing intense stress. Corporations are struggling, and in many cases failing, to meet the challenges of computer technology. Even in a growing economy, corporate downsizing has become so common that it doesn't even make the news most of the time. Middle managers, sacked in midcareer, wander through job searches like lost ghosts, hoping against hope that this is just a temporary setback. Wherever you look, the business news brings tidings of great change.

No industry has been harder hit than the computer industry itself. The decline of the traditional computer business can serve as an object lesson for what's happening to businesses around the world. The once-respected giants of many industries are suffering (even as the traditional computer vendors suffered) from upstart competition arising in unexpected places. Managers and leaders in every industry need to cope with, and take advantage of, massive market change. Here are some examples:

- *Telecommunications.* The rapid computerization of telephone switching, coding and decoding of optical signals, and miniaturization of orbital satellite components has fragmented the telecommunications industry. This has made it possible to deregulate the telephone industry, allowing local service providers to compete with giant national corporations. This trend will continue as the Internet becomes an alternative vehicle for voice transmission.

- *Broadcast Media.* Computerization rapidly reduced the cost of video editing and broadcasting, making it far cheaper to create and deliver video entertainment. Once dominated by a handful of studios and networks, the entertainment industry has fragmented in associated clusters of businesses, mega-empires comprised of small teams that have virtually complete creative control over the content that they produce. The Internet is driving further changes, as radio and television moves onto data links and digital video disks.

- *Automobile Manufacturing.* The globalization of the automotive industry—with parts manufactured and units assembled in multiple countries around the world—was made possible by the communications capabilities provided by computers. Even today, the increased computerization of manufacturing lines is making it possible to eliminate entire steps in the manufacturing process, entirely changing the nature of automotive assembly work.

- *Book Publishing.* The computerization of the writing and production process created a proliferation of competing imprints. At the same time, the computerization of warehousing and book ordering has caused the average bookstore order to diminish as retail outlets move to a just-in-time inventory model. Publishers are now assessing the impact of the Internet on the publishing business, as online services like www.amazon.com change the way the people purchase books.

- *Agricultural Chemicals.* The advent of computerized inventories in chemical warehouses has made it possible to radically reduce waste. Some companies are now trading excess inventories in order to increase profits. The resulting business model is radically different from the one that was common just a few years ago, a fact that's creating a new set of industry leaders.
- *Healthcare.* Computerization has become an absolutely critical element in the tracking and payment of healthcare. HMOs, for example, depend heavily upon computerization of all organizations levels in order to manage the process of dispensing and control healthcare resources. The Internet will provide additional ways for patients to purchase both insurance and healthcare.
- *Aerospace.* The process of building and manufacturing aerospace equipment has become completely dependent upon computers at every stage of research and development. Companies have been working with the government to establish criteria for the interchange of essential data, allowing products to be constructed from parts generated by hundreds of companies around the world. This has opened up new opportunities for smaller vendors, even as the larger vendors struggle through complex mergers.

The consistent thread among all these examples of massive market change is the computerization of the workplace. Fifteen years ago, the most sophisticated piece of technology on the average worker's desk was a telephone, a device that's been around for a hundred years. Today, nearly everybody in the typical office copes with personal computers (PCs), fax machines, voice mail, cellular telephones, networks, electronic mail, mobile computing, the Internet, and all the paraphernalia of modern computer technology. Work everywhere has become more hectic, more frenzied, as information and ideas fly around the "wired" corporation with the speed of light.

Not since the Industrial Revolution of the nineteenth century has there been such an explosion of new technology. And it all happened in the space of a decade. It's amazing how quickly all this new technology has disseminated into our lives.

How big an impact is computerization having on your industry? To assess this, take the quiz on page 15. It will allow you to assess how vulnerable your industry is to the kind of market changes that have transformed the entire computer industry. It will also help you assess how valuable the book could be for you and your organization.

The fact that major changes in technology have an enormous impact on business and economies should come as no surprise. During the Industrial Revolution, the "explosion" of technology took place over a period at least ten times longer. Even then, the social changes that resulted were massive—a complete transformation of the ways people worked and lived. For example, in the rural, agrarian culture that preceded the Industrial Revolution, few people worked regular hours. Many workers made the bulk of their income as temporary help during harvest and planting. Other workers plied trades, such as weaving or blacksmithing, that allowed them to toil at their own speed. Workers were either tied to the land or extremely mobile, going wherever there was demand for their services.

This seasonal style of working, while appropriate for a primarily agricultural society, was inappropriate for the burgeoning factories of the Industrial Age. Factory workers had to be present during scheduled hours for a factory to function effectively. During the early years of the Industrial Revolution, factory owners were plagued by workers who continued to behave like farmhands. Employees would come and go as they pleased, disappearing after payday and reappearing after their money ran out. This was such a serious problem that there were laws requiring regular factory attendance. Over time, the need for a prompt and reliable workforce created the modern industrialized city. The entire society had to adapt in the face of the new technologies.

Major changes in technology demand major changes in culture. In a global sense, culture, not technology, has determined which nations have prospered. Much of the technology

Answer the following questions True [T] or False [F]:

1. Many of the companies in my industry are undergoing massive internal change. [ ]

2. My industry couldn't function without lots of computer power. [ ]

3. We have, or could have, suppliers and customers anywhere in the world. [ ]

4. The time it takes to get a product to market is half what it was ten years ago. [ ]

5. Outsourcing (hiring outside firms to do inside work) is becoming common in my industry. [ ]

6. The competition generally knows what we're doing and vice versa. [ ]

7. A lot of people in my industry now communicate through e-mail and the Internet. [ ]

8. The sheer number of products that my industry handles has radically increased. [ ]

9. My industry has recently seen the entry of a set of new, start-up competitors. [ ]

10. Large companies keep buying smaller companies in my industry. [ ]

Scoring: Score 10 for each True answer.

Score 70–100. If your industry scored in this range, then it's clearly in the midst of a massive upheaval similar to the one that wracked the computer industry in the 1980s. For you, this book is a survival guide.

Score 40–60. If your industry scored in this range, then it's likely that changes are accelerating and that, within the next two to three years, your ability to succeed will depend on knowing exactly how the rules are changing. For you, this book is a planning guide.

Score 0–30. Relax. Your industry remains firmly in the machine age and is unlikely to experience the kind of massive changes that require the techniques described in this volume. For you, this book is a dandy paperweight.

of the Industrial Revolution was invented in China—gunpowder, movable type, accurate clocks, just to name a few. However, these innovations fell on the sterile ground of a highly traditional agrarian culture that was unable, or unwilling, to take advantage of these breakthroughs. Even after the Industrial Revolution had transformed the rest of the world, China continued to lag. Attempts to impose industrial technology onto the traditional culture initially proved disastrous. Mao Tse-tung's Great Leap Forward, for example, attempted to turn rural villages into backyard factories, a quixotic effort that not only failed to turn China into an industrial power, but ruined its existing economy.

The lesson of history is clear. Certain cultures are better suited to take advantage of advanced technologies than others. This ability (or inability) to take advantage of technology is likely to manifest itself in the culture's choice of leaders, and the development of its political structures. A culture can get trapped in a Catch-22 where it not only lacks the ability to adapt to new technology, but remains shackled in highly conservative institutions that almost reflexively fear anything new—especially technology that might enable or drive massive social changes.

What was true during the Industrial Revolution is also true today. For years, futurists such as Alvin Toffler have been talking about an information revolution—a change in technology that is as significant and fundamental as the Industrial Revolution of the nineteenth century. According to this theory, the world is undergoing a profound transformation away from the industrial economy of the past. In an industrial economy, wealth comes from the ability to control money capital. Markets change slowly, favoring large and stable corporations. In an information economy, wealth comes from the ability to manipulate and control information. Markets change swiftly, favoring nimble and adaptable corporations.

Just as China's conservative culture was unable to adapt to the Industrial Age, many corporations have business cultures that are ill-suited for the swiftly changing markets of the information age. Weighed down by bloated bureaucracies and hordes of middle managers, many corporations can't move fast enough to remain competitive. Executives and middle managers continue to cling to their hard-won authority and privileges. Employees dig in their heels and torpedo anything that seems to threaten the status quo. As a result, corporations continue to flounder, barely coping with the chaos.

This became clear to me when I discussed the history of the computer industry with Mitchell Kertzman, CEO of Sybase, a company that makes database software for personal computers and networks. I asked Mitchell why he thought IBM had failed to maintain its position of leadership inside the computer industry. He told me that it was *culture* that made all the difference:

> IBM simply got too bureaucratic to be nimble when technology changed. Today, technology changes so rapidly that you need a flexible, agile, nimble culture and management. If your culture is bureaucratic, you will not succeed in technology—period. You won't catch the waves. It's like an ocean liner trying to surf. The waves aren't going to move you, you're not going to see the currents, you're not going to catch the waves. You have to be much lighter and much more agile. IBM had a strong culture, but it eventually worked against them when the market changed.

Thus, in the computer industry, at least, the most powerful and successful companies were originally those that were highly centralized and autocratic, IBM for one. By 1990 or so, all of that had changed. Relatively decentralized companies, including Microsoft and Compaq, had overtaken their more centralized competitors. *Something* must have changed inside the business environment to make decentralized companies into more effective competitors than the centralized companies that preceded them.

Discovering that "something" has been the primary focus of the last few years of my life.

My Personal Experience

In my twenty or so years working in the computer industry, I had watched the great drama unfold. I'd experienced some of the pain and dismay that resulted from the Humpty-Dumpty tumble of the traditional vendors. At the same time, I had been privileged to work with the upstarts from the beginning of their rise to power and prestige. The contrast I saw between the old and new drove me to discover the secret of what it really takes to be successful inside these fiercely competitive markets.

I buried myself in the voluminous literature about management, reengineering, and corporate change. I coordinated million-dollar market research projects to discover the inner workings of the computer industry. I talked with hundreds of insiders, from chief information officers (CIOs) in corporate boardrooms to computer geniuses in advanced laboratories. I spoke at industry conferences and listened to what the other pundits had to say.

Finally, I decided that the only way that I could learn the real secrets of success would be to convince the people who led these successful companies—people like Bill Gates (Chairman of Microsoft), Eckhard Pfeiffer (CEO of Compaq), and Michael Dell (CEO of Dell Computer)—to coach me on what it takes to create a powerful and flexible organization. I also knew that these large companies were in some ways unique, so to broaden my investigation I spoke to a number of young entrepreneurs who were working to build their companies into the next big winners in the marketplace. My goal was to find the commonality between the management styles within the fastest growing segments of the computer industry. The result of this effort was a hardback book that came out with the rather daunting title *Business Wisdom of the Electronic Elite* (Random House, 1996).

It's been a whirlwind experience since then. The book gathered positive coverage in a host of major publications, including *The Wall Street Journal,* MIT's *Sloan Management Review, Worldbusiness, Industry Week, Government Executive,* and a large number of computer-related publications. The book captured the imagination of the broadcast media, resulting in personal appearances on *National Public Radio* and *NBC/Talknet* as well as numerous coast-to-coast television programs. The book was selected by three major book clubs and was selected by Soundview Execution Book Summaries as a top business book for 1997. The book has been translated into eight languages and is now available around the world.

As for myself, I found myself in demand as a professional speaker to corporate audiences hungry to learn about these cutting-edge management techniques. In fact, there was so much interest from the broader business community that my publisher and I decided to expand the book beyond its original focus, making it both more comprehensive and easier to use. The end result is the book that you hold in your hands. This book, like its prior version, is a compilation of the most effective management techniques gathered from high-tech companies around the world. It is based on the coaching that I received from the management geniuses who created this new corporate culture.

So who are these management geniuses? Some, like Bill Gates (Chairman of Microsoft) and Mitchell Kertzman (CEO of the Sybase database tools company), are college dropouts. Others, like Masayoshi Son (CEO of Softbank, the world's largest high-tech trade show company) and Eckhard Pfeiffer (CEO of Compaq, the largest manufacturer of personal computers), are from other countries. In general, these people are younger than the typical CEO. Michael Dell (founder of Dell Computers) is in his early 30s. Hewlett-Packard's Lew Platt in his mid-50s is the eldest of the group. I call them the "Electronic Elite," because they're the "best of the best" in high-tech management.

Their diverse backgrounds, however, do not mean that these leaders have nothing in common. Nothing could be further from the truth. What unites them is a new way of thinking about business that is very different from the conventional wisdom of the Industrial Age. When you listen carefully, you discover that these new leaders don't sound like typical dyed-in-the-wool-suit executives. They use different words, draw different parallels, apply different imagery. There's a restless dynamism about them that's hard to resist. They don't act frightened when confronted with new ideas. They have a very different mindset than the executives of the past.

Unlike the executives who run the traditional computer companies like IBM, Digital, or Unisys, this new generation of business leaders are highly creative entrepreneurs who've energized the modern computer industry. The Electronic Elite bring a unique quality of leadership to the business world. They've created organizations that are wildly productive and yet humane in their treatment of employees. Their companies look different and feel different from the typical corporation. Bureaucracy is almost nonexistent. Janitors hobnob with vice presidents. There's an egalitarian energy that inspires employees to try to change the world. The Electronic Elite have discovered how to create organizations of astounding creativity and flexibility. They are true role models for the managers of the future, not just in the computer industry, but in other industries as well.

I considered it a privilege to be instructed by these experts. And naturally I made certain to ask each one of them the question that had plagued me for so many years: *what was it that allowed a group of upstart companies to take over an entire industry from some of the wealthiest and most successful corporations in the world?*

This is the answer that they gave me: *"We created a new kind of business culture."*

What Is Silicon Valley Culture?

A new business culture was born in Silicon Valley, in 1939, with the foundation of a company known as Hewlett-Packard (HP). Back then—as in many corporations today—conventional business wisdom was that well-run corporations were "machines" and good executives ran them "by the numbers." It was considered smart to pay employees as little as possible, reducing them in the process to faceless, replaceable cogs.

The founders of HP, Bill Hewlett and Dave Packard, had a different idea. They believed that a corporation would be more productive if the employees also benefited from a corporation's success. Rather than building a corporate machine, they created a community of individuals, held together by a profound sense of mutual respect. As a result, HP has tended to avoid the centralization and bureaucracy that goes hand-in-hand with traditional business thinking.

Since then, Hewlett-Packard has grown to become the second largest computer company in the United States. The consistent, long-term growth of HP provides abundant proof that the best way to compete in a fast-paced business environment is to create a business culture that values freedom, initiative, and fun rather than obedience, conformity, and fear.

This new way of thinking naturally led to new management techniques—some of which have been widely adopted, even outside the computer industry. For example, in the past, many companies insisted that managers be treated with exaggerated respect. It was "Yes, Sir!," "No, Sir!," and "Right away, Mr. Jones, SIR!" Communication was tainted with fear. Employees rarely felt safe speaking the truth. At Hewlett-Packard, that was never the case. The founders were—by their own insistence—

Dave and Bill to their employees. Relations between managers and employees were casual, communicative, and productive.

Another management practice that's widely used today is "management by objective." Dave and Bill were among the first business leaders to promote this concept. Long before business schools even figured out there was such a thing, Dave and Bill were articulating that managers should set objectives, but give employees great freedom in the way those objectives were to be accomplished. By contrast, in organizations that have very tight control, you usually find that the top management is always trying to tell employees exactly how things should be done. Individuals aren't trusted. Freedom is automatically suspect. Micromanagement prospers and productivity plummets.

For many years, this new, team-oriented culture remained a peculiarity of Hewlett-Packard. However, in the late 1970s, the culture began disseminating outward into a number of small start-up companies, and remote divisions of established companies. The culture grew and took form until it became a completely new way to approach the management of any organization. I call it the "Silicon Valley business culture."

But I'm getting ahead of myself. It's impossible to exactly describe Silicon Valley culture without first explaining what a business culture really is.

The Roots of Culture

Back in 1984, one of the books being discussed in corporate America was *Corporate Cultures* (Addison-Wesley, 1982). This book explained how an organization's culture predetermines its employees' behavior. Authors Deal and Kennedy defined business culture as "a strong system of informal rules that spells out how people are to behave most of the time."

Corporate Cultures focused on "values" as the primary element of a business culture. The authors believed that the most important values of a culture were encapsulated in a corporation's motto. For example, the motto "IBM means service" reinforced IBM's dedication to the customer. The problem with this definition is that it doesn't explain why a company chooses a particular motto in the first place. Corporate mottoes are symbolic manifestations of a corporation's culture, but they don't define what the culture is all about any more than *E Pluribus Unum* explains what the culture of the United States is all about. To really understand business culture, we have to dig deeper.

A large part of any corporation's culture consists of the cultural mindsets that people use to evaluate the appropriateness of business behavior. A cultural mindset is a habitual image, metaphor, or paradigm that acts as an emotional and intellectual touchstone for determining what's "the right thing to do."

I like to envision business culture as the banks of a river. The behaviors in the corporation are like water that flows alongside those banks. Over time, these behaviors dig the channel deeper, reinforcing the culture so that it continues to reproduce the behaviors that led to success in the past, as shown in Figure I.1.

To understand the concept of a cultural mindset more clearly, it helps to look outside the business world for a moment. For

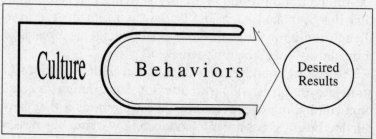

FIGURE I.1   *Culture Predetermines Behavior*

the past twenty years, the U.S. government has been waging a so-called war against drugs. The phrase "war on drugs" is a specific manifestation of a cultural mindset that considers social action to be similar to the process of conducting warfare. This Social Action = Warfare mindset also finds expression in phrases like a "war on poverty," and a "war against illiteracy." The warlike nature of this cultural mindset appeals to our sense of urgency. It's intended to suggest to people that their elected officials will spare no effort to "win the war."

However, the Social Action = Warfare mindset carries some unintended baggage. In the war on drugs, couching antidrug activity in terms of militaristic attitudes sets the tone for the debate about the problem. It forces our society to focus attention on warlike "solutions," such as the funding of special police forces, stepped-up efforts to catch offshore smugglers, defoliant bombing of South American drug fields, and so forth. The warlike metaphor also virtually guarantees that comparatively little attention will be given to less warlike approaches to the problem, such as drug education and therapy for addicts. It also keeps our government from seriously considering alternative approaches, such as decriminalization.

Decriminalization may be a very bad idea for a number of reasons, but as long as the debate is framed inside a Social Action = Warfare mindset, the idea is almost unthinkable. Decriminalization would seem like "surrender," an admission that the "war" had been lost. This would remain true even though the ultimate goal—less social damage as a result of drug abuse—might be thus achieved.

The cultural mindset of a corporation limits the kinds of strategies that it is willing to attempt. For example, a common cultural mindset in traditional corporations is that conducting business is similar to conducting warfare: Business = Battlefield. You see this mindset in action when you hear people say things like "nuking the competition" or "shooting the messenger" or "mustering the troops." Companies that have internalized the Business = Battlefield mindset are irresistibly drawn toward large, hierarchical, army-like organizational structures. Managers in such organizations are highly unlikely to effectively implement a scheme that requires low-level employees to make more decisions. Even though they may talk about "empowerment," managers in militaristic business cultures will tend to resist any attempt to turn employees into something other than "troops" whose business it is to "follow orders."

I once sat in on a meeting during which a consultant was presenting a reengineering plan to the management of a highly conservative, regimented, military-style corporation. One of the key points of the presentation was that the reengineering effort would "empower people." When the consultant began talking about this, the managers became restless and uncomfortable. The senior executive in the group stopped the presentation. "What exactly do you mean by empower people?" he asked the consultant. The consultant, sensing that he'd made a gaffe, thought quickly: "It means that the reengineering will empower management," he replied coolly. "After all, managers are people, too." At this, the audience relaxed into their chairs and listened to the rest of the presentation with open hearts and minds, because it didn't conflict with the unexamined belief that employees were supposed to follow orders.

Traditional Business Culture

The Business = Battlefield notion is an example of a traditional corporate mindset. I consider it to be traditional because the Business = Battlefield idea evolved when factory owners during the Industrial Revolution needed a way to coordinate the activity of large numbers of people. The most effective model for this in the nineteenth century was the Napoleonic army.

Napoleonic armies were controlled by a core of senior *officers*, had strong *chains of command*, dressed soldiers in standardized uniforms, and carefully segmented the activities of the *troops* into specialized functions. Early corporations mimicked these techniques—most corporations today are run by executive *officers*, have strong *chains of command*, insist that the *troops* wear blue collars, and remain obsessed with job titles and job responsibilities.

The Business = Battlefield notion is one of eight key cultural mindsets that underlie the traditional business culture that's prevalent in most companies today. It is familiar to anybody who's worked in or around "big business" in the past fifty years. Traditional business culture is symbolized by three-piece suits, fancy boardrooms, complicated organization charts, and a manage-by-the-numbers attitude. The eight key business mindsets summarized here include:

1. *Business = Battlefield.* Business is a series of conflicts between companies inside a market, between departments inside a company, between groups inside an organization, between individuals in a group and (by extension) between customers and vendors. Resulting behaviors: Managers build big empires and "armies" of employees to fight the war. The troops wait around for "marching orders," until managers order the "troops" around. Customers become territory to be conquered rather than potential partners, and the competition is demonized into the "enemy." Women, not believed to be natural soldiers, are considered inappropriate for positions of authority.

2. *Corporation = Machine.* An organization is a system in which employees are faceless cogs. Nobody is indispensable, and everybody is as replaceable as a spare part. Individual initiative, goals, and desires are considered to be completely subsumed by the demands of the corporate machine. Resulting behaviors: Managers create rigid teams with rigid roles and rigid functions. Managers and workers

alike become convinced that change is very difficult, similar to re-tooling a complicated machine. Managers are encouraged to think of themselves as "controllers" whose job it is to make sure that people follow the rules of the "system." Employees are treated in dehumanizing ways while the corporation centralizes control at the top.

3. *Management = Control.* The real job of the manager is to control employees' behaviors so that they do exactly what management wants them to do. Employees who disagree with a manager or refuse to do something are "insubordinate" and therefore dangerous. Resulting behaviors: Managers create organizations that can't adapt to new conditions because there are conflicting power structures, each of which is trying to "control" the corporation. Management gets involved in a supercharged political atmosphere where productive work becomes difficult. Individual initiative is killed in favor of a "let's-wait-and-see-what-the-boss-says" mentality.

4. *Employee = Child.* Employees are too immature and foolish to be assigned real authority and simply can't be trusted. If not restricted by complicated rules and regulations, they'll steal a company blind. Resulting behaviors: Employees develop a deep and abiding resentment toward management. They refuse to do anything until they're certain that they won't get blamed if something goes wrong. Employees spend more time "covering their butts" than doing productive work. Employees only work when they're being watched, if then.

5. *Motivation = Fear.* Employees only work because they're afraid of getting fired. Managers must therefore use fear—fear of getting fired, fear of ridicule, fear of loss of privilege—to motivate people. Resulting behaviors: Employees and managers alike become paralyzed, unable to make risky decisions or take courageous action. Work becomes a loathsome experience filled with truckling, ass-kissing, and compulsive corporate politicking.

6. *Change = Pain.* Change is seen as complicated and difficult. Change is considered something that companies only undergo if they are desperate. Resulting behaviors: Reengineering, restructuring, and downsizing operations fail as people in the organization torpedo the change efforts to avoid the pain of change.

7. *Computers = Masters.* Technology is seen as a way to strengthen management's control over the rest of the company. Employees become dehumanized into mere attachments to the computer system, the needs of which become far more important than the needs of the employees themselves. Resulting behaviors: Employees distance themselves from the corporate goals and may even indulge in sabotaging the computer system.

8. *Work = Toil.* According to this view, work, by its very nature, is something that is separate from the rest of life, a necessary evil that takes time away from the things that one would rather be doing. Resulting behaviors: People resent going to work and resent having to work. This resentment creates endless conflict between managers and employees who define themselves, respectively, as oppressors and victims.

These eight key traditional business mindsets are described in more detail later in this book. Most people in business assume that these traditional business mindsets simply reflect the "Way Things Really Are," when in fact these habitual ways of thinking are merely mental filters for interpreting business behavior. Just as the *Social Action = Warfare cultural* mindset limits how our government is willing to approach the drug problem, traditional business mindsets limit corporations to pursuing certain kinds of business strategies, even if those strategies no longer make sense under today's market conditions.

For example, if you've been reading the business press over the past ten years, you've probably seen the overwhelming evidence that centralized, monolithic organizations tend to be weaker and less competitive than decentralized, team-based organizations. In spite of this evidence, centralized, monolithic organizations often find it next to impossible to transform themselves into decentralized, team-based organizations, even though the use of well-regarded corporate change methodologies such as Total Quality Management (TQM). According to a recent poll cited in *Fortune* magazine, executives believe that less than one-third of TQM efforts are anything more than a "flop." The most frequently mentioned barriers to change were "employee resistance and dysfunctional business culture."

The consistent failure of corporate change attempts—even when change is desperately needed—makes sense when you understand the powerful influence that the eight key traditional cultural mindsets have on the subconscious attitudes of managers and employees alike. Any attempt to implement something like TQM is destined to fail if the management believes—at a gut level—that its function is to systematically use fear to manipulate the behavior of mentally inferior, child-like troops. Meaningful corporate transformation becomes even less likely if the people inside the dysfunctional organization are convinced—again, at a gut level—that any attempt to change the current system would be incredibly painful, involving loss of status, loss of salary, and (above all) loss of control. The subconscious influence of the cultural mindsets lock the status quo into place.

The effect of these eight traditional business mindsets is all the more pervasive because they reinforce one another, making it difficult to disbelieve in one without disbelieving in all the rest.

I was once called in to help a company decide how to organize to compete for a newly developing high-tech market. The company's highly successful competitors were structured into autonomous teams, with each team responsible for an individual product. This allowed them to bring products rapidly. By contrast, the company I was working with was organized into broad, functional groups with vague, bureaucratic responsibilities—an organizational structure that had enormous problems getting a product out the door at all, never mind quickly. Although the company I was working with had racked up a series of impressive failures, I encountered an extraordinary amount of resistance when I recommended a restructuring that would develop more punch to the product teams.

The first objective was, "our system doesn't work that way." When I pointed out that the system could be changed, I ran into the second objection, "Workers need management supervision." When I pointed out that the workers were, for the most part, highly educated professionals, the next objection was, "it would take too long to make major changes; we need to go after this market now!" When I pointed out that earlier attempts to address similar markets with its current structure had failed, I found myself back at the original objection: "Our system just doesn't work that way."

Trying to get that company to make necessary operational changes was like trying to cut off hydra heads—every time one objection was laid to rest, another sprang up to take its place. The reason for the intractable resistance was that its management was completely dominated by three business mindsets: Corporation = Machine, Employee = Child, and Change = Pain. Because of this highly emotional attachment, the company was unable to visualize or effectively implement the changes needed to be successful in its target market. Under the circumstances, the best that could be expected was an attempt to make current strategies more cost-effective. So rather than fixing the real problem, the company merely began a series of debilitating downsizes, which resulted in short-term profitability and long-term market failure.

Silicon Valley Culture

By contrast, some organizations have little difficulty adapting to new market conditions. In particular, companies that share the business culture of Silicon Valley have proven to be extremely nimble in this regard. To discover the reason for this, I had studied their organizational structure and business models, but I still wasn't able to put my finger on what was really different about these companies. I did know, however, that something had to be very different, because these companies were not only trouncing the traditional computer vendors, they were breaking major records for business growth and success.

Compaq, for example, shipped its first computer in 1982, and in 1983 (the year it went public), it recorded sales of $111 million—unprecedented growth for a start-up. Compaq then went on to top the $2 billion mark within six years. Dell Computers, run by boy-genius Michael Dell, grew from a $30,000 start-up in 1984 to a $3 billion corporation in ten years, making it one of the fastest-growing companies in the Fortune 500. Microsoft has done a truly spectacular job of creating wealth for its investors. Since it went public, Microsoft stock has been returning an average 59 percent yearly growth, enough to turn a $15,000 investment in 1986 into a cool $1 million by 1995. There was something unique about these companies and, by extension, something unique about the people who led them.

I've already mentioned that the Electronic Elite attribute the success of their companies to their powerful business cultures. During my conversations with the Electronic Elite, I started listening, very carefully, for clues that might lead me to identify the specific nature of this new culture. I began noticing that the vocabulary of the Electronic Elite differed from that of traditional business leaders. For example, in the many hours of business talk, I seldom heard the "shoot-em-up," "destroy the competition," "order out the troops" tough talk that had become so familiar to me in my contacts with top management of other corporations. Instead, these leaders used different words, drew different analogies, made different comparisons.

As I probed at their strategies and attitudes I began to perceive speech patterns that suggested business mindsets that were very different from the ones that provided the cultural framework for the typical "old school" company. I was able to see an important contrast between the traditional business mindsets (that I knew so well from my prior experiences) and the images, metaphors, and mindsets that the Electronic Elite were using. It eventually became clear that the Silicon Valley business culture represented a complete overthrow of the interlocked business mindsets that defined and delimited the business behaviors of the past. The new business culture represented a revolutionary new framework for business behavior, a framework that had evolved in response to the Information Revolution, just as the old business mindsets had evolved in response to the Industrial Revolution. These eight new mindsets are summarized here:

1. *Business = Ecosystem.* The business world is made up of symbiotic relationships formed to exploit market niches. The company that is the most diverse is the most likely to thrive. Business result: Companies adapt quickly to new market conditions, tend to hire and promote people with different backgrounds and thought processes, and form interesting partnerships with other companies.

2. *Corporation = Community.* An organization is a collection of individuals with individual hopes and dreams that are connected to their organization's higher purpose. Business result: Employees dedicate themselves to the goals of the organization and truly enjoy contributing to their own success, the success of their peers, and the success of the community at large.

3. *Management = Service.* A manager's job is to set a direction and to obtain the resources that employees need to get the job done. Management wants to "lead" rather than "run" the organization. Business result: Decision making takes place at the appropriate level of the corporation. Teams form their own rules and direction without interference from corporate headquarters.

4. *Employee = Peer.* Every employee is hired—regardless of position—as if he or she were the most important person in the company. Excellence is expected and encouraged everywhere from the loading dock to the boardroom. Business result: Employees at all levels take charge of their own destinies. A spirit of friendly competition develops to see who can serve the organization the best.

5. *Motivation = Vision.* People know where they're going and are amply rewarded when they get there, so the process of working is filled with energy, enthusiasm, and humor. Business result: Employees work hard, not out of obligation or out of fear, but because they believe in the organization's goals, truly enjoy what they're doing, and know that they'll share in the profits.

6. *Change = Growth.* Change is a desirable thing because it's part of the process of adapting to new market conditions and growing into new levels of success. Business result: Employees and organization embrace new ideas, new ways of doing business, and new ways of making profit.

7. *Computers = Servants.* Technology is a means to automate repetitive and boring work, thus freeing human beings to be creative and to build relationships. Business result: Organizations can learn faster and coordinate activities effectively.

8. *Work = Play.* Work is something that should be inherently enjoyable and the job of management is to help put people in jobs that will truly satisfy them. Business result: Employees tend to want to

spend time at the workplace, among their friends at work, doing the kind of things that they truly enjoy doing.

These eight business mindsets combine to create the cultural framework for companies that are decentralized, trusting, empowering, informal, and flexible, rather than centralized, bureaucratic, controlling, formal, and rigid. Just as the traditional business mindsets reinforce one another, Silicon Valley business mindsets are interlocked and mutually supportive. The Change = Growth mindset, for example, fits exactly with the notion that Business = Ecosystem. Similarly, the Employee = Peer mindset naturally leads managers away from controlling behaviors and into an attitude of serving the organization (Management = Service).

These eight cultural mindsets of the Silicon Valley business culture are described in detail in this book, along with the specific strategies to turn the new mindsets into competitive advantages. These mindsets (and the strategies they support) result in a productive, yet humane workplace that emphasizes freedom, initiative, and fun, rather than obedience, conformity, and fear. This new business culture represents a giant leap forward in the evolution of the American corporation.

The most significant difference between Silicon Valley business culture and the traditional culture of corporate business is that the new culture is much more egalitarian. It is no accident that the new culture evolved in a part of the United States that's known for being on the edge of social movements.

By contrast, traditional business culture has its roots in the European class structure. Silicon Valley culture is firmly grounded in popular American values and ideals. The Silicon Valley business culture, like that of the United States, sees itself as a meritocracy, where talent and hard work is more important than position or fancy titles. With its flattened management chains, free-form communication, racial/gender/ethnic blindness, love of diversity, widespread decision-making processes, and insistence upon individual responsibility remains profoundly American. And while the ideals of Silicon Valley, like those of the United States, are sometimes honored more in the breach than in the observance. Silicon Valley business culture represents a more democratic alternative to the autocratic organizations of the past.

This new business culture is being carefully imitated around the world, especially in Asia. Masayoshi Son is the chairman of SOFTBANK, the world's largest publisher of computer-related magazines and books, the world's largest producer of technology-related trade shows, and Japan's largest distributor of computer software and systems. Masayoshi's management style is clearly influenced by ideas developed by the U.S.-based high-tech firms:

There are many exciting companies in our industry, especially in the U.S. I personally get a lot of stimulation from speaking with Bill Gates or John Chambers (CEO of Cisco Systems) or Larry Ellison (CEO of Oracle). They're very visionary and very different, but they do have one thing in common. They all believe that this is an information revolution and truly believe in the future of our industry.

Companies that have Silicon Valley business cultures are far from perfect. Working in these companies can be frustrating. The hours can be long and there's often a great deal of internal competition. As in all human institutions, the reality sometimes falls short of the ideal.

Still, the people who work in these environments are, by and large, excited and fascinated by their careers. As I've spoken with the employees in these companies, I can't tell you the number of times I've heard, "I really love working here" or "this is a great place to work." And this isn't just from the executives, it's from the people who answer the telephones, program the computers, cart boxes to the loading dock, or field customer requests. This attitude seems strange indeed, if you're used to the rank-and-file griping that's typical inside the traditional, relatively oppressive organizations of the past.

This positive attitude reflects and reinforces the success that the companies of Silicon Valley have enjoyed as they've grown into some of the most powerful and influential companies in the world. Both the attitude and the success are the natural and inevitable results of the new cultural mindsets.

This book is your guide to the new culture and to the business strategies and tactics that are an integral part of that culture. It is organized as a learning tool, with each key to the new culture building on the one before. The description of each key contains:

- A description of each mindset, both old and new.
- At least one case study to show how the different mindsets affect business performance.
- A table to help you compare the old with the new culture.
- Specific strategies related to each key that you can implement inside your own teams.
- A quiz to access the level of evolution for your own organization.
- *Points to Ponder* to help you visualize how these new mindsets could positively impact your career and your team.

This book also includes an appendix summarizing the keys and the strategies. I've tried to make this book into a useful tool to help you make your teams more effective, emulating the ideas and actions of some of the most powerful and flexible corporations in the world today.

Key No. 1

Business Is an Ecosystem, Not a Battlefield

The Silicon Valley Mindset: Business = Ecosystem

The first and most important mindset of the Silicon Valley business culture is that the process of doing business is similar to guiding and directing the processes of nature: Business is like an ecosystem.

An ecosystem is a community of living organisms that have complex and finely balanced symbiotic relationships. While the members often compete for resources, they must always maintain balance. The death of a predator species, for example, might cause the destruction of an entire ecosystem through overgrazing by herbivores. Ecosystems that are homogenous—containing only a few species—are fragile. Any unusual event will upset the balance. Ecosystems that are diverse and contain a variety of species are robust and more likely to remain viable over long periods.

That's pretty much how the business world works. A market is a complex set of relationships between customers, vendors, suppliers, and competitors. These relationships are finely balanced and can include very large companies—like Microsoft—and very small companies, like your local computer store. Corporations can be regarded as ecosystems as well. Those that have a lot of biological diversity, a greater variety of people and products, are more likely to thrive than monolithic, single-product companies that are composed of people who think and act the same.

The Business = Ecosystem mindset is nothing new. The concept that economic systems paralleled biological systems had been bouncing around academia for some years before it was developed and described in 1990 by Michael Rothschild in the book *Bionomics: Economy as Ecosystem.* The Electronic Elite, however, are the first business leaders to take this new mindset entirely to heart.

One high-tech company that has an ecological view of business is Novell. When Novell was founded in 1980, it was a tiny organization making add-on boards for those few hobbyists who were building personal computers at the time. Novell soon began concentrating on software networks, the computer technology that connects personal computers. To remain competitive and to stay on the edge of technological innovation, Novell grew by acquiring and merging with other technology companies.

Rather than trying to create a single, monolithic organization, former Novell CEO Ray Noorda let these different businesses pursue strategies and tactics that made sense for their products. This gave the company a robust diversity that made it possible to adapt to changes in the marketplace. When economic conditions or technical breakthroughs rendered one Novell group less successful, another Novell group benefited. The strategy paid off. From a tiny start-up in 1980, Novell's 1994 revenues climbed to over $1 billion, and the company employed over 4,000 people.

Since then, the company has encountered fierce competition from Microsoft, competition that has dropped the company from the limelight. However, with a customer base in the tens of millions, Novell remains a significant player in today's computer industry. Bob Frankenberg, a former CEO of Novell, commented on why diversity is important to an organization:

If you become too homogeneous, you can become very introspective and find yourself without the diversity that's necessary for evolution when a market changes or when a new set of capabilities emerge. All of the studies of evolution point out that the diversity of a given population is one of the prime factors required for survival, and so, becoming too homogeneous is very dangerous. Novell has roots in twenty-three different companies. We have different ways of developing. . . . We've got a wide range of approaches. I think that if we don't continue to do that, as conditions shift (and in this business, conditions shift very frequently), there's a danger of not surviving; but most important, I think we would miss some of the great opportunities as they emerge.

When Bob talks about evolution and diversity, he's revealing the influence that the Business = Ecosystem mindset has on his strategic thinking. This mindset has allowed Novell to behave in ways that are totally foreign to run-of-the-mill traditional companies, which tend to view business as a battlefield.

The Traditional Mindset: Business = Battlefield

Many traditional business leaders have a militaristic view of the way the business world works. A glance at the titles of popular business books—*Marketing Warfare, Leadership Secrets of Attila the Hun, Guerrilla PR*—offer ample testimony for this widely held viewpoint. We're told that we must imitate generals and warlords if we want to be successful managers. Taking all this to heart, many executives talk as if they were planning the next world war:

This product will do major damage in the marketplace! We've armed our salesforce. We've targeted the right set of customers!

39

The new ad campaign will explode into the territories! This is going to be a major victory! Our troops are ready!

Yes, Virginia, some people really talk like this. And it would just be macho rhetoric if it weren't that it symbolizes a general attitude that's frequently ineffective in today's fast-moving markets. We really can't blame traditional executives for thinking this way because their beliefs are deeply embedded in their business culture. In the typical corporation, power is concentrated at the top, where the commander in chief (chief executive officer) is surrounded by a general staff (corporate officers), who give orders to lesser officers (vice presidents, directors, etc.), who give orders to the line officers (line managers), who give orders to the troops (employees). These orders *must* be obeyed; failure to do so (insubordination) results in court-martial (disciplinary action) or death (termination).

Although the analogies between business and warfare seem timeless, people didn't always connect them. In the Middle Ages, warfare was the occupation of dukes and princes, and only commoners and knaves soiled their hands with commerce. In fact, if you had suggested to a knight that business was the same thing as warfare, he probably would have gently corrected your by separating your head from your shoulders. In the eighteenth century, it was the other way around. Merchant princes hobnobbed with dukes and kings, while warfare was a dirty business best left to mercenaries, wastrels, and cutthroats.

Today, however, many companies resonate with warlike attitudes. And if a company's executives really believe that business is warfare, then that dogma will be reflected in nearly everything that goes on inside the corporation. Strategies that don't fit the dogma—regardless of their potential for success—will be rejected because they are literally "unthinkable." For example, executives who believe that business is a battlefield will almost inevitably assume that victory in business goes to the largest "army" and they'll build large, complicated departments full of people and resources. Even when customers would be better served by a smaller, more focused effort, there will be an overwhelming drive to build a massive corporate "army" that's "strong" and ready to "fight."

That was one of the problems that IBM had in the 1980s, according to former IBM vice president Willy Shih:

What most big companies need is more decentralization. The best structure is to become a collection of small businesses. That's hard for big companies, because executives don't want to think about anything that isn't a $100 million business. Yet that's exactly how Microsoft and Intel got started—as small companies. Big companies approach developing markets in exactly the wrong way. Since everything they're interested in is supposed to be a $100 million business, they invest in enough infrastructure to make it a $100 million business. But that's the last thing that you want to do, because now you have a cost structure that undercuts your profitability and a bureaucracy that keeps the business from adapting to the market.

In addition to building large organizational empires, military-minded managers find it all too easy to become control freaks. Because they see themselves as generals and officers, they *tell* people what to do. They think that good employees should shut up and follow orders. This behavior destroys initiative as people wait around for top management to make decisions. And because top management is often the most isolated from the customer, the company loses track of what's needed in the marketplace. Further, the Business = Battlefield mentality makes it impossible to put the decision making where it belongs—at the lowest level of the organization.

Military thinking also distances employees from their customers. To the militaristic company, customers are, at best, faceless territory to be "targeted" and "captured" with marketing and sales "campaigns." This strategy discourages the viewing of customers as living, breathing human beings with opinions, interests, and concerns of their own.

This attitude can deeply offend customers. On a recent plane trip, I sat next to the vice president of a large media company. He told me a story about a salesperson who had given a sales pitch for a new computer system. The salesperson kept using the word "targeted": The product was "targeted" for the media industry, the ad campaign was "targeted" at new customers, sales resources had been "targeted" in this geographic area, and so forth. Finally the vice president got fed up and threw the guy out. "I felt like he was aiming a gun at my head," the vice president confided to me. "Not once did he bother to tell me how his product would help me make more money."

Military-minded companies often abuse customers in their quest for "victory." Since "all's fair in war," they feel free to use any means—fair or foul—to "win." This was brought home to me when my mother, a top salesperson for a cosmetics firm, got a new manager. He was a typical corporate Rambo, forever giving the salespeople pep talks about "hating" the competition, "blasting them out of the water," and "doing major damage in the region." This tough talk translated into pushing distributors to order products that they didn't need so that the sales manager would have a "winning" quarterly report. The distributors, naturally, began to order less, which drove the sales manager crazy. He intensified his pep talks. One day he ended with the instruction, "So let's rape and pillage, and leave no wounded!" At this, my mother raised her hand. "Excuse me, sir, could you clarify a point, please?" "Certainly." "Who, exactly, do you want us to rape?" she asked, her voice dripping honey. She took early retirement a few weeks later.

Which brings up another issue. The whole military concept, with its buddy-buddy, band-of-brothers, shoot-'em-up consciousness seems ludicrous to many women. Not having spent their childhood playing soldiers in the sandbox, many women find it pretty ridiculous that a bunch of grown men can act as if their boring meetings and dry-as-dust ideas were high adventure and global conflict.

The militaristic organization almost always discriminates against women. From time immemorial, warfare has been a male pastime, and though women have often fought and died in wars, they're generally considered second-class soldiers. Men who think that executives should be generals in three-piece suits find it extraordinarily difficult to envision a woman in a position of power. This is shortsighted, because women are capable of the highest performance at all levels of business activity. Military thinking, which disqualifies women from being full contributors, weakens organizations by stripping them of a valuable source of new ideas and insight.

Leaders who have adopted the Silicon Valley business culture don't buy into the Business = Battlefield mindset because they know that it's inconsistent with the kind of business behaviors that produce success in today's marketplace. For example, Frank Ingari is the president of Shiva, a Massachusetts-based company that makes software for mobile computers, explained why he and many of his peers consider the Business = Battlefield mindset to be dysfunctional:

I simply won't tolerate disrespect of people. That's a basic value with me. If people have integrity and a sense of wholeness, then there's no excuse for treating each other with disrespect—sexism, ageism, any kind of discrimination, any kind of militaristic behavior. "I am the pooh-bah and I am ordering you to do the following things." I don't buy that at all. My disbelief in militaristic power doesn't mean that I don't use power. There are many times where I've said, "Hey, this is what we're going to do." But I don't just tell my direct report we're doing it and leave it at that. I'll call all the employees into a room, explain the rationale; I'll tell them everything. I'll tell them the financials, what I was thinking, my concerns, what I weighed, the decision I made, who's accountable for the decision—usually me—whether or not I'm open to entertaining any debate. So, it's not that you don't direct, but you treat people with respect even when you direct. My goal is that communication is not going to be to tell you that this isn't my fault, and you should just do what I'm telling you. I'm going to try to get you to understand why this happened, and if I take a black eye, well, okay, I'm human too. I'm going to make mistakes.

One of the few elements of the Business = Battlefield way of thinking that's still present in Silicon Valley companies are the military-style job titles (such as CEO). However, when a high-tech manager tells you that he or she is a vice president or chief technical officer, there's often a bit of a twinkle in the eye or a lift of one eyebrow, just to let you know that you shouldn't take the title too seriously. You get the impression that the typical high-tech leader would just as soon be called head gardener or chief cook and bottle washer, if it weren't that the financial community won't talk to you unless you have a fancy nineteenth-century title on your business card.

This is not to say that there aren't individuals and companies in Silicon Valley that don't sometimes use warlike talk. But such talk tends to have a strangely zen-like flavor to it. For example, Larry Ellison, the CEO of database software giant Oracle, has been known to quote Sun Tzu's *Art of War*, a treatise that recommends a completely bloodless conflict as the highest form of strategy. This is worlds away from the hard-ass industrial age CEO who sees himself as a latter-day General Patton.

With few exceptions, high-tech leaders far prefer the Business = Ecosystem mindset, which drives an entirely different set of business behaviors from the Business = Battlefield mindset, as shown in Table 1.1.

The behavior that's driven by the Business = Ecosystem mindset seems insane by those who hold the battlefield viewpoint. In an army, diversity makes for a rabble; starting small seems a recipe for getting crushed; and, in the end, what's a

TABLE 1.1
COMPARISON OF BATTLEFIELD AND ECOSYSTEM MINDSETS

BUSINESS = BATTLEFIELD

- *Uniformity.* A strong organization is one where everyone dresses the same, shares the same background, and follows corporate standards.
- *Cash Cows.* The primary goal of every organization is to defensively protect profitable revenue streams, even if it means foregoing new opportunities.
- *Conflict.* Business is essentially a win-lose proposition. It's a zero-sum game where competitors, and even customers, are enemies.

BUSINESS = ECOSYSTEM

- *Diversity.* A strong organization is diverse, containing a wide variety of opinions, ideas, products, and sales channels.
- *Generations.* The goal of every organization is to create new products, which make currently profitable products obsolete.
- *Symbiosis.* Business is a set of win-win relationships, not only between customers, vendors, and suppliers, but even among "competitors."

battle without winners and losers? Conversely, militaristic behavior is viewed as insane by followers of the ecosystem mindset. Uniformity means that organizations can't adapt; blitzing markets seems like pulling up young plants to make them grow faster; and conflict just seems like so much wasted effort.

The ecological mindset provides valuable insights into what really works in the Information Age. Companies that embrace this mindset find it easier to remain flexible, grow new businesses, and establish positive business relationships. Companies that remain tied to the Business = Battlefield mindset are naturally and inevitably led toward strategies that were more appropriate for the slow market cycles of the Industrial Age. This difference is shown in Figure 1.1.

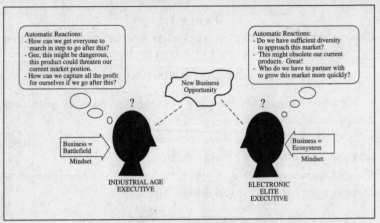

FIGURE 1.1   *Different Mindsets Drive Different Business Strategies*

The dominant mindsets inside an organization inevitably influence the way the people of that organization try to solve a problem or take advantage of a market opportunity. The battlefield mindset leads companies to behave in ways that may have made sense in the past, but that are recipes for failure today. To illustrate this, let's look at different ways that one high-tech company, Novell, and an older, more traditional minicomputer vendor, Digital, both attempted to dominate the market for computer networks.

Case Study: Novell and Digital
Strive for the Network Market

It was 1980. The personal computer was considered more of a toy for hobbyists than a viable computing platform, but exciting things were starting to happen in the computer industry. Unbeknownst to all at the time, the era of the centralized mainframe was drawing to a close, even though most computers that year were still large mainframes that sat safely inside temperature-controlled rooms at corporate headquarters. Anyone who wanted to access the precious computing resources of the mainframes had to beg corporate bureaucrats for rental time. To satisfy this growing need, IBM and the other mainframe manufacturers were trying to build *bigger* and faster machines, in the hopes that they would be able to serve a greater number of people.

At the same time, another group of computer vendors were building minicomputers, scaled-down versions of the giant mainframes. Unlike the mainframes, which required a special environment, minicomputers could be installed virtually anywhere. This meant that an individual department or division could purchase its own computer, making it unnecessary to access the computers at corporate headquarters.

Digital Equipment Corporation (Digital) was the unquestioned leader in minicomputer technology. What made Digital's computers particularly useful was that they were easy to configure into networks. This meant that the computers in different departments not only could share data, but could cooperate with each other to solve difficult computing tasks.

There were many reasons why Digital's networking idea made sense. Networking allowed companies to distribute computer power away from corporate headquarters. People at a manufacturing center, for example, could keep track of inventory using a computer that was located inside the plant. This computer could, in turn, be connected to another machine in the accounting department that helped the purchasing department order supplies; which then could be connected to a third computer, on which engineers could design the next product to be manufactured. The network freed people in different parts of the company to own their own "departmental" computer while still sharing important data with other departments.

Networking minicomputers had advantages over the giant mainframes. If the mainframe had a problem, all the departments and divisions that depended on it would lose their access to computing power. A system crash or other error could easily cause havoc throughout the entire company, bringing productivity to a gut-wrenching halt. With a Digital-style network, on the other hand, if one of the computers had a problem, the rest could continue to function; only the department with the "sick" computer suffered. While this might prove inconvenient to the affected department, it was certainly less likely to bring the entire company to its knees. In many cases, people in the affected department were able to use the computers in the other departments while their own computer was getting fixed. Thus, a Digital network could be both safer and more cost-effective.

Enter the personal computer. The PC, with its built-in microprocessor and communications capability, was the perfect vehicle for creating new computer networks. Just as Digital's minicomputers had made it possible to build networks, the personal computer made it possible to build low-cost networks using even smaller components. This made many of the advantages of the Digital-style network available to a much larger group of people, and at a much lower cost.

Here was a once-in-a-decade opportunity for Digital, and if the company had rewritten its networking software so that it would run on the personal computer, Digital could have captured the rapidly growing market for PC-based networks. Digital was, after all, the acknowledged leader in networking software. Other computer vendors had competing products, but none of them were as flexible, useful, practical, and stable as those that Digital made. Digital also had hundreds of thousands of loyal customers who would have flocked to buy a PC network built by Digital.

Digital did not respond to the challenge, however. Rather than embracing the personal computer and rewriting its software to run on them, Digital clung to its minicomputers. It made some half-hearted attempts to include personal computers as part of their minicomputer-based networks, but that wasn't what customers wanted. As a result, despite Digital's dominance of the networking market, Novell was easily able to capture market share to the point where, today, Novell owns two-thirds of the market for networks. Digital, once the market leader, wanders around in the basement with single-digit shares.

How could Digital, which practically invented networking, become so irrelevant, so quickly? What happened was an almost classic series of blunders on Digital's part, and Novell grew at Digital's expense because it approached the business of making money in a very different way:

- *Business Model.* Novell, like Digital, had originally been a hardware vendor. However, Novell began focusing on software when it became clear that it was more profitable to sell software than hardware, even though this required a major change in Novell's business model and method of operation. Digital, on the other hand, continued building and selling hardware based on the same business model that they'd been using for the past twenty years. Novell's culture was flexible; Digital's was not.
- *Product Strategy.* Although the sales figures for personal computer networks were initially small, Novell stayed focused on this market niche, believing that it would continue to grow over time. Digital, on the other hand, continued to tap what it regarded as the more established market for minicomputer-based networks. This limited the appeal of Digital's networks to those people who wanted to buy Digital's proprietary products. Novell's culture searched for growing market niches; Digital's languished in a dying one.
- *Channel Strategy.* Digital sold the majority of its networks directly to customers, providing them with hardware, software, installation, and support—a "one-stop shop." Novell, on the other hand, concentrated on software, which it sold through value-added resellers (VARs)—local, privately owned companies. Where Digital tried to capture all the profit for itself, Novell shared the profit with its small-scale partners. Novell's culture encouraged this kind of symbiotic relationship; Digital's tended to exclude outsiders as if they were "enemies."

Novell adapted to new market conditions, while Digital kept doing the same things that had made it successful in the past, even though they were no longer producing success. Digital's inability to adapt wasn't the result of management stupidity; the company had recruited the brightest and best from the leading management schools. And it certainly wasn't caused by a lack of technical expertise; Digital was filled with engineers such as David Cutler, who today is the architect of Microsoft's advanced networking operating system, Windows NT.

If it wasn't a lack of management brainpower or technical expertise that caused Digital to blunder so consistently, what was it? The answer is that Digital suffered from staying in the confines of a business culture that was not evolving apace with the fast-moving markets of the Information Age. This rendered Digital's management incapable of making the kind of clever moves that the upstart Novell found so natural. Digital was constrained by cultural insistence on viewing networking in one way. Digital's culture didn't provide the framework for a Novell-like strategy; instead, it limited its managers' choices to strategies that had worked in the past but that proved increasingly ineffective as time went on. Even when the ineffectiveness of the ingrained system was amply reflected in Digital's declining profitability, the company continued to do the same things, pursuing the same strategies, like a clockwork doll on overdrive.

Digital essentially was hypnotized—and thus crippled—by the Business = Battlefield way of looking at the world. For example, it was not unusual in the Digital of the 1980s for managers to give presentations that featured pictures of tanks, battleships, and fighter planes meant to represent different products, companies, and organizations. Military vocabulary permeated the company. People didn't design marketing strategies, they "launched campaigns." These campaigns had militaristic names like "Rolling Thunder" (named after the bombing campaign during the Vietnam War) or "Top Gun" (named after the popular movie). And this kind of talk wasn't limited to managers. Among the "troops" (workers were always "troops"), it was popular to say that a person who had been criticized during a meeting had been "blown away," "massacred," or "nuked out of existance." A common greeting in the hallway was "how goes the battle?"—a greeting often accompanied by fingers shaped in the form of guns and aimed at one another.

The warlike images, vocabulary, and hand gestures were surface manifestations of the internal processes of the organization. Given the fascination with the battlefield mindset, it was inevitable that Digital would evolve toward ever more bureaucratic and stable organizational structures, with direct lines of command and executives who were determined to "run" the company.

Indeed, that is exactly what happened at Digital. The company's 1980s management opted for an organizational structure in which all the employees with a particular expertise were grouped together. Thus, there was a massive engineering group, a massive marketing group, and a massive sales group, each responsible for *all* of Digital's products and services. Under this kind of organizational structure, Digital employees naturally felt that their primary loyalty was to their functional discipline. Getting products out the door became secondary to making certain that corporate rules and regulations were followed.

During the critical years that it was competing with Digital, Novell was enjoying an organizational structure based on the ecosystem mindset. Each product group had the resources and decision-making power to go after the market for that group's products. Rather than trying to *control* the process, Novell's top management *coordinated* activities and encouraged peer-to-peer cooperation between product groups, as shown in Figure 1.2. This allowed Novell employees to look at

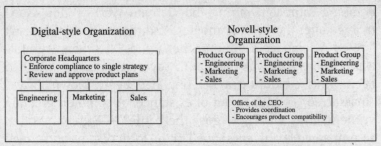

FIGURE 1.2   *Battlefield and Ecosystem Organizations*

the market in a way that made them more nimble, more flexible, and better able to take advantage of opportunities and market changes. Former Novell CEO Bob Frankenberg commented:

> If you looked at some of the older computer companies or some of the ones that haven't made the transition, what you saw were these giant hierarchies. That was one of Digital's problems, for example. It had a functional organization, and all of the development was in one organization, all of the marketing was in another. Faster, more fleet-footed competitors, who structured themselves into small businesses yet stayed tied to the right kind of communication and information systems, were able to outrun Digital.

Implementation Strategies

In addition to promoting different organizational structures, the Business = Ecosystem mindset encourages companies to follow three important business strategies. Understand these strategies and why they're effective and you'll be that much closer to making the power of the ecosystem mindset work for your organization. These strategies are:

- Encourage diversity.
- Launch new generations.
- Build symbiotic relationships.

Let's see how these strategies work in the real business world.

STRATEGY 1: ENCOURAGE DIVERSITY

Earlier in this chapter, we learned how Novell's former CEO Bob Frankenberg values the diversity of an organization. He sees Novell's different businesses as important to Novell's future survival. Participating in a number of different businesses, with a variety of business models, makes Novell a stronger company, according to Bob. It makes the company far less likely to be damaged by a major shift in market trends and provides fresh alternatives for making money. Bob explained:

> I have a strong belief in what I call tight and loose. A few things are held very tightly but a lot of freedom is given to do what's needed. One of the tight elements is a set of objectives that we agree on. We come to agreement on what we're going to accomplish in each of the business groups. The other thing that we consider important is having the communication abilities to move information around so bright people can make good decisions based on the best information that we can get to them. We treat people with respect and hire the very best people. Beyond that, we've got a wide range of approaches.

Thus, while Novell's strategic direction comes from a "big picture" view of where the company needs to go, the implementation details, business model, and approach are determined by the people responsible for executing the specific parts of the overall plan. Novell maintains diversity, while being focused enough to keep from straying into inappropriate or unprofitable markets.

The devotion to diversity spills over into the kind of personnel decisions that they make. When you visit the companies in Silicon Valley (or anyplace where the Silicon Valley management style is practiced), you immediately notice that they are filled with people from different social, racial, and cultural backgrounds. This is no accident, nor is it the result of altruism or a sense of social conscience. On the contrary, the effective high-tech leaders value personnel diversity because they know that it's critical to the continuing process of innovation.

One company with a history of innovation is Lotus Development Corporation. Lotus grew to be one of the largest software companies in the world by selling what was once the most popular personal productivity software of all time—the 1-2-3 spreadsheet. Jim Manzi was the CEO of Lotus during its most dramatic growth years. I asked Jim how he viewed the issue of diversity in the workplace. His response was, in my opinion, acutely representative of the way that the effective high tech leaders perceive this important issue:

> *I have no interest in being politically correct, which I find basically an obnoxious concept. However, there is a shared point of view at Lotus that a diverse culture—meaning people of different backgrounds and particularly people with different cognitive skills—makes for a better corporate culture, better products, and better service. These people bring different perspectives to a common problem, as opposed to having cookie-cutter white men of the same age and cultural background. A diverse culture is a lot more interesting for everybody, and this reflects in the kind of products that get built.*

It's difficult to imagine a viewpoint that's further from that of the traditional CEO. In general, corporate America has had to be dragged kicking and screaming into accepting diversity.

Despite years of apparent progress, the glass ceiling remains a formidable barrier to people who don't fit the mold of the white male leader.

Companies that have a Silicon Valley business culture don't have to be convinced with quotas and arm-twisting to accept a diversity of personnel into the workplace. On the contrary. They *embrace* it. For them, the issue of diversity isn't one of fairness or some other moral abstraction. Diversity is a survival issue. Companies that want to be successful can't afford a uniformity of thought that's so characteristic of the traditional corporation, because it's the kiss of death in today's quick-changing marketplace.

Being successful in the Information Age requires a very creative company building exciting new products quickly and effectively, forging new sales channels in a matter of months, and helping customers discover new ways to use new products. Just as the most robust ecosystems are those that contain the greatest variety of lifeforms, the most creative companies are those that enjoy the greatest diversity of viewpoints.

Another indication of the commitment to diversity is the relatively high percentage of key management positions held by women in these companies, considering the fact that engineering is traditionally a male-dominated field. For example, two of the most important software companies in the industry (AutoDesk and Ask Computing) are headed or were founded by women. That's something that's not true of any other industry, with the possible exception of the cosmetics industry. Furthermore, it's extremely common to see women in senior vice president roles or running major divisions inside high-tech organizations. And, increasingly, women are starting their own high-tech companies.

Ann Winblad was one of the first women to found a software company. In 1976, Ann cofounded Open System, Inc., a top-selling accounting software supplier. Beginning with a $500 investment, she operated the company profitably for six years and ultimately sold the company in 1983 for $15.1 million. Since then, she's been a mentor to an entire generation of software CEOs, including Microsoft Chairman Bill Gates. Ann pointed out that of the dozen or so companies she featured in her latest brochure, three had women as CEOs or cofounders. But she pointed out:

> *The fact that they were women had nothing to do with the decision. The software industry is a meritocracy. We back the people with the best ideas.*

That's exactly how Silicon Valley views diversity. They hire the best people, and the best people are those with a fresh perspective.

Getting back to Novell, the company very wisely abandoned networking hardware in favor of a focus on networking software, even though this meant changing their entire business model, and not just because software was cheaper to manufacture and had higher margins than hardware. Novell software was designed to run on personal computers supplied by many different hardware vendors. When the cost of personal computer hardware dropped, it created an enormous demand for accompanying software. Novell was positioned perfectly to take advantage of this trend, and it was able to make the move into software because its management included people from different backgrounds and different companies. From the start, it was a diverse company, composed of many different people with a variety of ways of viewing the computer industry.

Digital's managers, on the other hand, clung to their tried-and-true business model. Most of Digital's management had been trained to design, manufacture, and sell hardware. Digital's management lacked the diversity of opinion and experience that would have enabled them to see future opportunities and accept the challenge to alter their way of doing business.

Digital's management, consciously or unconsciously, was culturally driven toward greater regimentation, resembling the army that it was using as a model for good business practice.

Digital's executives, for all their brilliance, were cut from the same cloth. Novell, by contrast, with access to the softer and more flexible ecosystem mindset, had a tradition of encouraging diversity. This stood them in good stead when they needed to change their business model to take advantage of new opportunities.

There is another aspect of making the most of opportunities; having the right product at the right time. To achieve this, a company must utilize another ecological strategy, allowing a new generation of products to become prominent when the time is right.

STRATEGY 2: LAUNCH NEW GENERATIONS

In an ecosystem, lifeforms survive through a process of reproduction. Each generation begets the next generation, thus ensuring the survival of the species. There's a cycle to life, a growth and decline of each generation. Companies with a Silicon Valley culture view their products in much the same way. They see products as having a relatively short lifetime, believing that even the most successful product of today is destined to be replaced by a next-generation product.

Carol Bartz is the CEO of AutoDesk, a wildly successful California-based software company that makes the world's most popular computer-aided design (CAD) package. As the head of one of the largest personal computer software companies in the world, Carol is arguably the most powerful woman in the computer industry. She's also a leader in public opinion and acts as a role model for many women in the computer industry. Carol explained the all-important notion of generations in high-tech products:

You can't be afraid to obsolete your current products. You have to be very aggressive about taking a winning product and being ready to declare it obsolete, just when it's started to win. For example, in the hardware business, before you even introduce your product, you have to be readying its cost-reduced version simultaneously. If you don't, by the time you get around to engineering the cost-reduced version, your competitor will have done it for you! Advanced technology is spread around in so many places that it's not possible for a company to control it all. You can't set the direction and, therefore, you can't really control your future. You have to give up on that concept, and you must go into the market knowing that other companies' technological advancements are setting the route for you.

Effective managers know that their current product is destined to be replaced, either by a product of their own or by a product from a competitor. What's more, they realize that the new product may be very different from their current product. It may use a totally different technology, or it may be sold and marketed a completely different way. Effective managers, when they see the market about to shift, are not afraid to sacrifice their old products in favor of new ones. To the contrary, often they replace their current products long before the market knows that it "needs" a new generation.

This attitude differs significantly from that found among traditional computer vendors who, like many other companies, tend to be terrified of abandoning a currently profitable product in favor of something new. That's exactly what happened at Digital in the 1980s. It was more concerned with protecting the market territory it had already captured than with entering into new businesses, especially those that might threaten its current revenue.

Throughout the 1980s, it was clear to most people in the computer industry that the personal computer would eventually be capable of performing the computing tasks that were currently being implemented on minicomputers and main-frames. The personal computer represented the new generation of computing. Novell fully understood this and decided to concentrate on building networks for this new generation of computers.

STRATEGY 3: BUILD SYMBIOTIC RELATIONSHIPS

Symbiosis, a concept that Silicon Valley has borrowed from ecology, is the process by which two or more organisms of different species cooperate to enhance their ability to survive. In an ecosystem, symbiotic relationships often develop between species that might normally be enemies. For example, there's a variety of bird in Florida that forages for food in the open mouths of alligators. The alligators get their teeth cleaned and the birds get a free lunch. The two exist in a state of symbiosis, providing mutual benefit.

Most traditional organizations treat relationships as a zero-sum game, where there are always winners and losers, just as there would be on a battlefield. The notion of mutualism or symbiosis is never considered. That's why so many traditional companies try to capture all the profit. The motto of the Industrial Age manager is "never leave money on the table." In this game, the winner is the company or person who extracts the most profit from every situation. This attitude precludes different companies from working together because somebody has to lose in order for somebody else to win.

The concept of symbiosis, by contrast, permits more complex relationships between organizations. One of the major reasons that Novell was able to grow a profitable networking business was that it developed symbiotic relationships with the small, independent dealers that sold and installed Novell's software. This arrangement allowed Novell to concentrate on what it did best—building great software—and let the independent dealers concentrate on what they do best—remaining close to the customer and providing the service needed to make the networks run smoothly. Novell and the independent dealerships created a state of symbiosis that's been profitable for both.

Leaders inside Silicon Valley-style companies are always searching for win-win symbiotic situations. This permeates their business deals, their attitude toward their employees, and even, to a certain extent, their relationships with their competitors. These companies often find it profitable to partner *and compete* with the same companies. This phenomenon is so common that a new word has been coined to describe this business behavior: *co-opetition.*

Let me give you an example of how this works. Microsoft sells the popular Windows operating system software that runs on IBM-style personal computers. The main competition for the Windows/IBM PC combination is Apple's Macintosh personal computer. Apple and Microsoft are continually vying for market share, a competition that has been going on for many years. But Microsoft and Apple aren't just competitors, they're also business partners. How can this be? Microsoft also sells the most popular word processer and spreadsheet programs for the Macintosh, so obviously, without Microsoft, fewer people would be buying a Macintosh; and without Apple, Microsoft would lose part of its highly profitable applications software business. The two companies are involved in co-opetition—competing in one realm and cooperating in another. This would be impossible if Microsoft and Apple viewed each other as implacable enemies. Apple and Microsoft executives can't afford to take this narrow, militaristic view of the situation.

The rest of the business world, on the other hand, finds it difficult to see Microsoft and Apple except in terms of implacable enmity. That was why so many people were initially confused when Microsoft decided to make a $150 million investment in Apple in the summer of 1997. Far from destroying Apple, Microsoft was helping to keep the company afloat—something that only made sense for Microsoft, which saw the Apple platform as a source of profit and market growth for Microsoft's applications.

Despite their reputation for cut-throat dealings, most successful high-tech companies aren't obsessed with the idea of destroying the competition. Their primary competitive motivation is positive—they want to grow a business and increase the overall size of the market. Sometimes, they even cooperate with companies in the same marketplace to "heat up" the market—so that *everyone* makes more money.

Sally Narodick, former CEO of Edmark, a Seattle-based company that develops and publishes educational software and print materials for early childhood and special education students, talked about the way her company approached business:

> We're in a ballgame, and we get to play in a ballgame that is in this rapid growth phase. Here is the game plan: We've got to do extremely well, clear as a bell in front of everybody, and we celebrate our successes on that. And our game plan is to carve a very different niche and position for our products relative to the competitors.

Sally used the ecosystem mindset to visualize a niche where her company can grow and prosper, which freed her company from the shackles of win-lose and zero-sum.

The ecosystem mindset provides the groundwork for symbiotic relationships that strengthen their companies' positions and help to grow the demand for innovative products. Is it any wonder the companies in Silicon Valley (and their similarly minded brethren around the world) also find it so easy to outmaneuver, outdevelop, and outsell the overregimented behemoths of the past?

How Evolved Is Your Organization?

The following quiz will allow you to assess how far your organization has assimilated, or is free of, the traditional values of corporate militarism.

••

The Following Is True . . .

	Always	Frequently	Sometimes	Seldom	Never
1. I hear the buzzword "chain of command."	___	___	___	___	___
2. People here have different life experiences.	___	___	___	___	___
3. Our executives tend to dress alike.	___	___	___	___	___
4. We adapt quickly to new opportunities.	___	___	___	___	___
5. Our managers tend to think alike.	___	___	___	___	___
6. Women have equal advancement opportunities.	___	___	___	___	___
7. Our employees are called troops.	___	___	___	___	___
8. We partner easily with other companies.	___	___	___	___	___
9. We passionately hate our competitors.	___	___	___	___	___
10. We have easy, open relationships with customers.	___	___	___	___	___

••

Scoring:

For all odd-numbered statements, score:

Always	1
Frequently	2
Sometimes	3
Seldom	4
Never	5

For all even-numbered statements, score:

Always	5
Frequently	4
Sometimes	3
Seldom	2
Never	1

If your score is 10–20: Corporate militarism is a major thread inside your organization. People tend to wait to follow orders before taking action. Conflict and turf wars are common among top management. While the organization may be successful today, it may be difficult to make changes to adapt to new conditions.

If your score is 21–35: Your organization is average. Conversations in meetings sometimes lapse into macho tough talk, but it's not always a dominant theme. Managers and executives are allowed to approach problems in different ways.

If your score is 36–50: Your organization is close to the Silicon Valley ideal. Decisions are made at all levels of the organization, without the constant need for management approval. Relationships are generally considered more important than rules and regulations. You adapt quickly and easily to new market conditions.

Points to Ponder

In order to create leverage for change, write out the answers to the following questions:

- How has this corporate militarism been a help or a hindrance in your current marketplace?

  _____
  _____
  _____
  _____
  _____

- What kind of "new blood" would make your organization more diverse and therefore more adaptable? And how would you make such a change possible?

  _____
  _____
  _____
  _____
  _____

- Would your organization be willing to make its own products or services obsolete if the market changed rapidly?

  _____
  _____
  _____
  _____
  _____

- How much more profitable would your organization be if you easily formed symbiotic relationships and partnerships with both customers and competitors?

_____

_____

_____

_____

_____

The Business = Ecosystem mindset is the first key to create a powerful and flexible business culture. However, it's not just how you view the business world that predetermines success, it's also how you view the purpose and direction of your own organization. That's the reason behind the second key to Silicon Valley culture . . .

Key No. 2

···

CORPORATIONS ARE
COMMUNITIES, NOT MACHINES

···

The Silicon Valley Mindset:
Corporation = Community

Everyone knows that Microsoft has made millionaires of hundreds of its employees. Less commonly known is that many of these millionaires continue to work at Microsoft after they've achieved financial independence. That probably sounds crazy to you, especially if you're one of those who insists "If I win the lottery, the first thing I'll do is tell my boss to take this job and shove it." Certainly, for most people, becoming wealthy would be a ticket to quit. But evidently some of the Microsoft millionaires don't see it that way.

This phenomenon of the devoted Microsoft employee is more exceptional when you consider that Microsoft working conditions aren't easy. Sixty-hour workweeks aren't uncommon, and when there's a major product release, workweeks move into the triple digits. Microsoft isn't known for great employee perks, either; on the contrary, Microsoft is notoriously thrifty. For many years, Chairman Bill Gates drove himself to the airport and flew coach class when on Microsoft business.

So, what would cause a bunch of millionaires (not to mention a billionaire or two) to stick with such demanding jobs longer than was economically necessary? The answer is simple:

it's the sense of community, of belonging to something greater than the self. The corporation has a very deep sense of community. People there feel as if they belong to something special. Here's what Microsoft Chairman Bill Gates said about the culture he helped to create:

> *Our corporate culture nurtures an atmosphere in which creative thinking thrives, and employees develop to the fullest potential. The way Microsoft is set up, you have all the incredible resources of a large company, yet you still have that dynamic small-group, small-company feeling where you can really make a difference. Individuals generate ideas, and Microsoft makes it possible for those ideas to become reality. Our strategy has always been to hire strong, creative employees, and delegate responsibility and resources to them so they can get the job done.*

This sense of community is not unique to Microsoft. Companies with a Silicon Valley culture are obsessed with creating a similar sense of belonging in their organizations, which deepens the work experience and adds value to the lives of employees. One articulate spokesperson for the Corporation = Community mindset is Frank Ingari, CEO of Shiva. I asked him how companies like Shiva inspire the kind of loyalty that brings out the best in their employees. Frank told me:

> *The need to collaborate with a group to create a product taps into something really deep in the human psyche. It might have something to do with the breakdown of the family. Today, you don't have the shared sense of life experience with family and community the way you once did. We're no longer a band of pioneers moving to America. Neither are we a band of farmers raising our children together in the fields of Sicily. We don't have that any more. We're all nuclear families, if we're even in families at all. Because we're so alone, there's something really deep that wants you to tap into a shared effort.*

It's human nature to want to belong to something greater than the self. One of the most common ways to achieve this is to associate with people with whom you share a common interest. That's increasingly difficult in today's fragmented world, where families are constantly being uprooted and moved from place to place. Because ties to geographic communities have been weakened by our nomadic society, it's only natural that people should turn to the workplace to satisfy this important human need.

After talking to Frank, I was somewhat troubled. I wondered, were the managers taking advantage of their employees, using the loneliness inherent in modern life as leverage to get people to work harder? To Frank, though, satisfying this need for connection is a vast improvement over the dehumanizing work environments so common in Industrial Age corporations. Frank commented:

> We provide people with the opportunity to experience the positive aspects of collaborative work. I really believe in trust and diversity and empowerment, and when to back off and when to press on. These things are really important in people's lives. After all, we spend more time with our colleagues than we do with our spouses.

To Frank, the Corporation = Community mindset is a matter of *satisfying* rather than *exploiting* a basic human need. Effective high-tech firms want the individuals in their organizations to extract more than just money from their work experience. They want people to enjoy what they're doing.

Don't misunderstand: These companies don't encourage this sense of community as an act of altruism. On the contrary, this is a very practical matter. The nature of competition in the Information Age requires workers to spend long hours at work. Effective managers know that people won't work as hard if they aren't enjoying themselves and attaining some personal as well as professional satisfaction. It's essential that they feel they are surrounded by people they trust and who share the same goals. In other words, sustained productivity is difficult unless employees feel that they're part of a community.

Few companies, however, can also be considered communities. Instead, many people in business today—executives and employees alike—are far more prone to think of their companies as gigantic machines, which is unfortunate, because the Corporation = Machine mindset has some seriously detrimental consequences.

The Traditional Mindset:
Corporation = Machine

James Champy, in his 1995 book *Reengineering Management: The Mandate for New Leadership,* writes that one reason many companies have become uncompetitive is that "modern day management thinking" is based on the notion of the "corporate machine." Champy points out that economic conditions have made this view of the corporation an anachronism, and that the behaviors, such as the centralization of power that the metaphor encourages, now constitute a recipe for failure.

Despite this, the Corporation = Machine mindset is still popular. Listen to the way executives talk and business authors write about corporations. A successful corporation is often said to be a "well-run" or even a "well-oiled machine"; it also is said to be a "good system," one that is "efficient" and "well-designed." When you hear these descriptions or hundreds of others like them, you're hearing the Corporation = Machine mindset at work.

The Corporation = Machine notion implies that corporations can be improved by changing the "design" of their processes, just as you might rework the inner mechanism of a complicated machine. Ironically, the word "reengineering" can throw a mental roadblock right in front of any attempt to change a corporation. Machines are, by nature, rigid; a good machine is stable, orderly, and organized. Machines never grow; they never change on their own, except when they break down due to sheer age or improper care. When you want to change a machine, it has to be reengineered to do something different, which is, by definition, a long and costly process.

If you think of a corporation as a machine, then changing it is like taking a jackhammer to a steam engine. You might be able to create something useful out of the fragments, but it is unlikely. To the machine-minded executive, corporate change is always sacrificing something that works in favor of the un-known. How many corporate change efforts have been de-railed by the cliché "If it ain't broke, don't fix it"? This might be good advice for an automobile mechanic, but it may not be the best way for corporations to adapt to new market conditions.

Furthermore, machines need to be "run." The Corporation = Machine mindset encourages top management to visualize themselves in the control room of a big machine. Executives who think this way inevitably find if difficult to let people make their own decisions. This mindset can make top man-agement feel powerless as well. The CEO of Xerox once con-fessed to a friend of mine:

> I feel like the captain of an aircraft carrier. I turn the wheel and try to point the ship in a new direction, but I have no idea whether or not my orders are being followed.

Managers who think this way can't *lead* an organization because they're too busy trying to *run* it. One of the most de-bilitating effects of the machine mindset is the way that it de-humanizes people. Nobody is essential; anybody can be replaced. What's important is the "system," the great machine, how well it's run, how well it's "engineered" or "reengi-neered." Naturally, any corporation where this mindset is rampant will not reward creative thinking or recognize the value of intellectual differences. People who feel they're just part of a machine aren't going to go out of their way to help an organization achieve its goals. In the worst case, they might be tempted to exact some kind of revenge on the company that's treating its employees like subhumans. When organizations treat employees like cogs in a wheel, work slows to a crawl. People do the minimum, just enough to keep from getting fired.

In organizations with a Silicon Valley business culture, the opposite is the case. Because their employees view of themselves as leaders of a community, rather than controllers of a corporate machine, they find it easier to get people connected to the organization's larger goals. Table 2.1 identifies the differences between the two approaches.

TABLE 2.1
COMPARISON OF MACHINE AND COMMUNITY MINDSETS

ORGANIZATION = MACHINE

• *Dehumanization.* The system is more important than the individual. People are merely cogs in the corporate machine.

• *Elimination of Labor.* The perfect corporation consists of a CEO pulling the levers in a factory that has no people, only machines.

• *Alienation.* Employees feel disconnected to the goals of the organization and, therefore, do the absolute minimum required to "get by."

ORGANIZATION = COMMUNITY

• *Humanization.* The individual is more important than the system. People provide the creativity and drive that creates profit.

• *Career Development.* Education and training increase the value of the community to the marketplace.

• *Connection.* Employees develop a deep loyalty to the higher goals of the organization, and make an extra effort to turn the dream into a reality.

To understand the value of the Corporation = Community mindset, let's re-examine a story that's an archetype for the vast changes that the computer industry has undergone. It's a David versus Goliath story of how a wet-behind-the-ears college kid built a multibillion-dollar company that captured major market share away from one of the largest and most respected companies in the world. It's also a story about how a community can overcome a machine by keeping people in touch with the higher goals of the organization.

Case Study: IBM and Dell Compete in the PC Market

Earlier in this book, I gave an overview of the story of the growth of Dell Computer, promising to explain how and why Dell was able to do so well in the face of entrenched competition. To understand how this growth took place, we'll need to look more closely at founder Michael Dell and the business conditions of the time.

During the years the microprocessor was first being built into computers, Michael Dell was a teenager in Austin, Texas. Michael was interested in microprocessors and thought that there might be a business opportunity there. Nevertheless, this notion wasn't developed enough to keep him from seeking a college degree in a field that had little to do with computers or technology.

At the same time that Michael Dell was sifting through his freshman class schedule, a thousand miles away in Boca Raton, Florida, a new division of IBM had just been formed. This division was mandated to create an IBM product based on a microprocessor. This product came to be known as the IBM Personal Computer, the IBM PC.

IBM's PC division was not a typical IBM organization. It was heavy on engineers and light on the professional managers that ran the show at corporate headquarters. And it was no accident that the PC division was located in Boca Raton. The heads of this new division knew that if they were going to produce a product in record time, they had to be as far away as possible from the corporate bureaucrats and "quality police."

The IBM PC wasn't a typical IBM product, either. IBM's mainframes were made of hardware and software parts that had been constructed by IBM. The *proprietary* focus of IBM's mainframe and minicomputer design resulted in unique products that were difficult for a competitor to reproduce. This made a great deal of sense at the time of their development because it helped lock customers into using equipment from IBM—and *only* from IBM.

The PC, on the other hand, was constructed out of pieces and parts from other manufacturers. The central processing unit (CPU) chip—the brains of the computer—came from a little-known company called Intel. The operating system—the software that tells the CPU how to "think"—came from a backroom start-up by the name of Microsoft. This product "openness" meant that, unlike previous IBM products, the IBM PC could be *cloned* by other manufacturers. There was nothing to stop you or me from building an imitation IBM PC in our garages, a fact that was not lost on some future multi-millionaires.

But constructing the IBM PC from spare parts not only was expedient (it sped up the development process), it also made good business sense. Even though competitors could imitate the IBM PC, IBM could set the standard; in fact, by keeping the PC open to imitation and competition, IBM helped ensure that it became the standard, giving IBM a favorable market position as the demand for personal computers grew. True, IBM would never be able to dominate the market for PCs as it had dominated the market for mainframes. But if IBM had not built an "open" machine, it would have had to design all the parts itself rather than purchase them from other manufacturers. This would have taken time that IBM didn't have. A long delay for an IBM entry into this market would have allowed Apple or some other competitor to capture so much of the market that IBM would have remained outside the market completely.

Eventually, a vast armada of IBM PCs captured the infant market. IBM's PC division was positioned perfectly to grow as the market grew. And grow it did. By 1987, the total sales of IBM PCs reached $6.5 billion, making IBM's PC division, by itself, nearly two-thirds as large as the second largest U.S. computer company at the time (Digital). IBM captured fully 25.5 percent of the personal computer market, dwarfing Apple, which was limping along with a meager 10.5 percent.

Then disaster struck. Don Estridge, the "father" of the IBM PC, was killed in a plane crash. It was Estridge who had helped convince IBM's top management to give the PC division the autonomy it needed to develop such an unconventional product in such a short amount of time. His death was an enormous blow to the morale of the PC division's employees who had worked so hard to make the PC a success. Further, it seemed to sound the death knell of the PC division's autonomy. The success of the PC inevitably caused IBM's bureaucrats to descend on the PC division like a plague of blue-suited locusts. The division's management was transported to New Jersey, where it would be closer to corporate headquarters, and subject to review and tighter supervision. The days of radical innovation were gone.

IBM's management tried to implement strategies that would have made sense 10 years before, but that were hopelessly obsolete in the world of the microprocessor. IBM assigned bureaucrats and quality engineers to oversee the follow-on product, the IBM PC-AT. It was 18 months late and flawed by a brittle hard drive that had a tendency to break unexpectedly, losing all the customer's data. Next IBM tried to put a stranglehold on the growing market by creating a proprietary standard for plug-in boards to augment the capabilities of PCs. But the other PC manufacturers refused to cooperate, further eroding IBM's leadership position as the pacesetter for PC design and implementation.

These blunders might not have proven so serious had IBM's mainframe group not seemed determined to make life difficult for the PC division. Rather than accepting the inevitable—that the microprocessor meant the end of the mainframe—IBM's mainframe proponents were determined to protect their turf, even if it meant that IBM's PC business would suffer. In effect, the mainframe group waged a war of silence against the PC, refusing to admit that the new device was making their mainframes obsolete. One former IBM vice president told me:

When I worked in IBM's mainframe business, I used to say that by the time the mainframe guys figure out that we're in trouble, it'll be too late. That was in 1987. What surprised me was the rapidity with which the decline came. The whole thing fell apart in months, where normally you would expect that kind of decline to take some number of years. There were a lot of people in the ranks who were predicting it, and there were a lot of people at the very top who understood that it was inevitable as well. So what was the problem? It was this big bubble of upper and middle management. Akers [then CEO] couldn't do anything about it because he became the leader of that pack, partly by working with them. They were his friends; he grew up with them in the company, in the culture. So when it came time to do hard things—like canceling projects and firing people—he found it too difficult. IBM was full of very highly educated overachievers who made it to high levels. Nevertheless, the company became dysfunctional, so dysfunctional that it became difficult to change.

Meanwhile, back in Austin, Michael Dell was splitting his energies between his freshman classes and "wondering what to do on the weekends." Almost as an afterthought, he began selling add-on chips and disk drives that worked with IBM's

PCs and the many compatible brands that were becoming available at the time. Michael obtained these components from the same companies that supplied IBM; however, because Michael had virtually no overhead, he could sell them much more cheaply by mail than IBM could sell them through direct sales representatives. By 1984, his dorm-room business was grossing $80,000 a month. Michael branched into full-blown IBM-compatible PCs, selling them through the mail at a 40 percent discount over IBM's prices. The fledgling Dell Computer began to grow swiftly, often selling to the very customers that IBM was neglecting. Within ten years, Dell Computer was the fifth largest manufacturer of personal computer systems. IBM, on the other hand, had tumbled to number four, squandering its original 25.5 percent market share into a pitiful 8.5 percent share.

IBM once had a truly great PC division, as creative and innovative as any company in the computer business today, which it ruined with micromanagement and bureaucracy. Conversely, Dell Computer has grown to be a large company, but without the bureaucracy normally associated with a large company.

We could write off the success of Dell Computer as a fluke, but the Dell story is not unique. The computer industry is full of upstart companies that have trounced massively entrenched competition. For example, few people, even inside the computer industry, had ever heard of Microsoft before the personal computer exploded onto the scene. Add to that, companies such as Compaq, Gateway, Packard Bell, Acer, the list goes on . . .

There are many reasons that Dell Computer and the rest of the PC companies were able to steal market share away from IBM. One was that Dell had lower overhead and thus could sell computers at a lower price. But that's only the veneer atop the real story. Dell Computer had lower overhead because its employees were more productive than those at IBM. Why?

One reason was that CEO Michael Dell believed in the value of a sense of community in his organization.

Now in his 30s, Michael Dell is one of the most successful entrepreneurs of his generation. Boyish and irrepressible, he brings enthusiasm to the job of running a Fortune 500 company. Michael reiterated the importance of community in the success of his company:

> *People look to the company as a place where they want to build a career and a life, and not as a place where you come for a little while, then leave and go somewhere else. We definitely want to build that sense of belonging and being a part of something. And, with a company like this, that's growing rapidly, there's every opportunity to do that, and I think you'd be really foolish not to take advantage of that kind of enthusiasm and excitement in the people who are building what we expect will be a great company.*

IBM destroyed the feeling of community that had been forged at the Boca Raton plant; its top management believed that to make the PC division more productive they had to integrate it into the larger corporate machine. At IBM, the vision of the corporate machine made IBM blind to the reality that it's people who make products successful, not a system. A former IBM top executive told me:

> *I've spent thirteen years of my life inside large public institutions like IBM, where an individual doesn't really matter. You quit, they replace you. You move from job to job. You're an interchangeable part. It's left over from the Industrial Age, and it's wrong, and I hate it. It takes the value out of the individual. It's people who actually make these institutions work, not the system. There are people who want to blame the system for making people dispensable. It gives management a safer, more secure feeling. Somebody quits, no problem, we'll replace him. It's a socialist view of the world, and it's ridiculous. The individual is very important to*

success. Every interesting company and every interesting product is the creation of a few individuals. Period.

Silicon Valley culture rejects the mechanistic notion of the corporation; for them, the corporation is a community, and they take a lot of pride in the communities that they create. Mitchell Kertzman, CEO of Sybase, commented:

One of the great satisfactions of having built this company is having something that I started myself. Now that we employ hundreds of people, we have social events, we see all the families and the children. There are a lot of human beings involved in this enterprise, and they're of tremendously high quality; they're fanatically committed . . . and they really believe in what they're doing. It's an amazing thing to have helped to put together something that people can feel so strongly and positively about.

Implementation Strategies

There are three business strategies that companies with a Silicon Valley culture use to create a sense of community:

- Communicate directly.
- Sponsor social events.
- Encourage hands-on charity work.

Let's look at each of these in more detail.

STRATEGY 4: COMMUNICATE DIRECTLY

In general, it's easier for small corporations to maintain a sense of community than large corporations. When all the people in an organization work together intimately on a daily basis, they're forced to communicate with one another, and a sense of community arises naturally. There's a feeling of shared goals and shared responsibilities. When people talk, they form social bonds; that's human nature. Communicating brings people together.

That process is more difficult in large corporations. People begin to lose track of who has joined the organization. Some move to remote facilities, making one-on-one communication difficult. If the organization isn't careful, growth may result in a loss of this all-important atmosphere. I asked Shiva CEO Frank Ingari how he would structure an organization so that it didn't sacrifice its community atmosphere:

> *There's no cookbook answer to organization, and the needs change over time; and there are many ways to organize. I absolutely want to retain the feeling of connectedness—it's difficult, though. The notion of connectedness to the corporation becomes more tenuous, more communications-oriented than physical and literal. In other words, in a company like Lotus, you're connected to Lotus by what you read in the press and what your in-laws read in the press. You're connected to Lotus by its image in the community, by its benefits package, and what your spouse thinks about how generous the benefits are. Those are very, very different things than being connected to Lotus because you got drunk with the CEO last night at the barbecue.*

Organizations and the people who lead them thus have an ongoing challenge when it comes to maintaining community in the organization, but it can be maintained if management pays attention. A company like Hewlett-Packard (HP) is proof that a company can maintain a high level of connectedness, even as it grows.

The key, according to Lewis (Lew) Platt (chairman of the board, president, and chief executive officer of Hewlett-Packard Company) is to use every means possible to keep the feeling of connectedness alive. Lew explained how he uses his role as CEO to create a sense of connectedness at HP:

> *I do a lot of traveling, close to two-thirds of my time, and I spend a lot of time in front of HP people. I do this in fairly informal ways—like wandering around one-on-one, just talking to people. Other times, it's what we call coffee talk—the coffee talk is pretty famous here at HP. We get everybody at the site together and have a half hour where we talk about what's going on in the company, what's important, what's ahead, and then take some questions from the audience. I usually tack a half hour or an hour at the end to do some mingling with the people. These things are very important.*

Lew's coffee talks aren't just public relations exercises. He actually listens to his employees and tries to incorporate their ideas into HP's corporate strategy. Through listening to and communicating with as many employees as possible, Lew shows he cares, and that permeates the entire organization.

Community building shouldn't be limited to live appearances. Electronic mail enables an organization's leaders to connect without actually traversing geographic boundaries, and even people working in remote sites around the world can feel that they're part of a corporate community. Shiva CEO Frank Ingari commented:

> *As a large company, you have to organize to maintain multiple levels of connectedness. Manzi [then CEO of Lotus] sends regular electronic mail to all his employees, you know. Somebody drafts those for him, but he crafts them himself. He edits them, and he's very concerned with what they say, and they come from his desk under his name. Gates does the same thing.*

As computer technology becomes more sophisticated, there are ever more opportunities and methods by which to connect. For example, at Sun Microsystems, a manufacturer of computer workstations, managers can send an electronic mail message to employees that contains a video clip that can be displayed right on their desktop computer screens. This allows managers at Sun to communicate their energy and enthusiasm immediately and directly to the employees.

STRATEGY 5: CREATE OPPORTUNITIES FOR SOCIAL INTERACTION

Direct and frequent communication, even when augmented by powerful electronic communication, is not, however, enough to maintain sense of community. Effective high-tech managers also make certain that there's plenty of face-to-face contact. One of the most effective ways is to create occasions for social interaction. Venture capitalist Ann Winblad explained to me how truly effective organizations make people feel that they are an important part of the larger organization:

> *They have functions for the new recruits, functions for the first-year recruits, functions for all the summer workers, and functions for Christmas. You're made to feel part of a winning team. I think that that prevents burnout. Work becomes a social experience as well as just a work experience, and I think that's driven from the top leadership. I think the companies that have the least amount of burnout have a team approach, which really makes everyone feel like they're not just a cog in the wheel.*

As Ann pointed out, Silicon Valley companies sponsor a lot of social mixers. These parties are extremely egalitarian and are used to increase the amount of communication and community feeling between managers and employees. That's a good idea, but it's one that many traditional corporations can't seem to fathom. I recently received the following description of a social event at a traditional corporation:

> *Our company organized its company picnic to improve company morale. At the picnic, there was a managers' table with steak and lobster. The employees' table had hot dogs and beans. As you might expect, company enthusiasm was not served.*

By contrast, many successful high-tech firms sponsor monthly or even weekly get-togethers so that people can connect to the organization. All levels of management are included, and everyone is encouraged to mingle freely. Michael Dell, CEO of Dell Computers, explained how this works:

> *Any kind of activity where you can get people together and communicate is very helpful for our business. You have to break down barriers and promote informal communication. You build friendships within the company, and people begin to understand that "those people aren't out to get me; we're all in this together."*

These social mixers need not be formal. For example, I once worked at a software development organization that had a tradition called a Quality Assurance (QA) Meeting. This semi-official meeting was held every Friday night at a local restaurant. Everyone was welcome, including spouses, children, and even former employees. These QA Meetings brought people from different organizations together, mostly to talk business, but also to discuss *Star Trek*, surfing, gardening, and many things of genuine concern to the corporate community. There was a free flow of information between organizations, managers, and employees.

Many times, these discussions ended in a burst of inspiration, and it wasn't unusual for a group of programmers to return to the office and work until the wee hours implementing something exciting, so that they could impress their colleagues when they returned to work on Monday. These QA meetings cost the corporation nothing because people paid their own way. However, meetings were, at least in part, responsible for a rate of productivity in that group that was twice the industry average.

Integrating families into the workplace is another way to foster social interaction. If the corporate community is to replace the more traditional forms of community, then it *must* include families. One high-tech leader who has come to this conclusion is Bill Gross, the CEO of Knowledge Adventure, a developer of multimedia software for children. Bill used to work at Lotus where he had a broad range of product development responsibilities. As a result, Knowledge Adventure has become a pioneer in the inclusion of families as part of the corporate community. Bill commented:

> *We integrate family life into the work environment in a variety of ways. I still try to do as much work as I can from home so I can be with my family. We also have a pretty open policy about staff bringing their families into the office, either after school or on weekends. A lot of us work on weekends, when there are a lot of kids around here playing. It's almost like a playroom for the kids, and they play with our products. We do, of course, have other things besides computers for them to pay with—building blocks, coloring books, Legos, and all that. Having the kids around while we work has been great. We can go out to lunch together, the kids get to know each other, the parents get to spend time with their kids, and the parents get to show their kids what they do for a living. I'm really proud that I can show David what we're doing here; and the other kids, I think, are very proud of what their parents do.*

One organization that accomplishes this very well is Hewlett-Packard Mexico. I recently taught a workshop entitled "Creating a High Tech Culture" to 400 of HP's most valued resellers during an HP-sponsored conference. The HP meeting planners included spouses and families in numerous events, including all the meals. There was an enormous feeling of community, symbolized by the name of the conference itself "Juntos" which means "Together" in Spanish.

The inclusion of the family into the work environment may represent a return of a earlier conception of the work experience. Before the Industrial Revolution, men worked where they lived, on the farm and in craft workshops. This meant that fathers participated regularly in the raising and teaching of the children, and were more deeply integrated in the family and community life than is generally possible in an industrialized society. Today, as more and more women enter the workforce, there's a real danger that they too will become as alienated from their families as men have been.

According to Kristin Lund, vice president of the Illinois-based Praise and Leadership Schools, Inc. (a company that consults with corporations on in-house preschool programs), numerous studies have shown that business productivity is greatly improved by the presence of on-site child care. There is less absenteeism, decreased tardiness, less turnover, and increased job satisfaction. It also makes it easier for parents to remain in the workforce without sacrificing frequent day-to-day contact with their children.

It's important to include children as part of the corporate community. That's why it's exciting to see companies like Knowledge Adventure or Hewlett-Packard Mexico where children are a welcome part of the environment. Far from making organizations less productive, this policy is likely to make people more dedicated to the success of the corporate community.

STRATEGY 6: ENCOURAGE
HANDS-ON CHARITY WORK

Another way that companies with Silicon Valley cultures promote social interaction is by sponsoring hands-on charitable
events. Charitable contributions have always been part of the
corporate scene, but the companies with a Silicon Valley culture tend to prefer small charities because they lend themselves to group activities, such as bake sales, benefit concerts,
and the like, which build a sense of community. Michael Dell,
CEO of Dell Computers, commented:

> *One thing I think has worked particularly well for Dell in Austin
> is that our workforce is very active in volunteer and community
> activities. We regularly sponsor volunteer fairs, and the com-
> pany, through its charitable donations, directs funds at those ac-
> tivities that employees participate in as volunteers. We poll our
> employees to understand what they're interested in and direct
> our funds toward those charities.*

This kind of charitable contribution connects people not just
to the organizations, but to the community at large, according
to Sybase CEO Mitchell Kertzman:

> *I grew up in the 1960s, so I'm an old left winger, but I'm not as
> liberal as I used to be. However, the notion that we should build
> businesses that are culturally positive is a great thing. It also
> means the opportunity to be charitable. My company's very in-
> volved in education. For example, we partnered with a middle
> school in a depressed neighborhood nearby. We helped the stu-
> dents set up their own business selling T-shirts they could learn
> leadership, entrepreneurship, and business skills. I like being a
> good corporate citizen, a good member of the community.*

When discussing this kind of charity work, it's important to differentiate it from the depersonalized United Way drive that's a hallmark of many traditional corporations. While United Way no doubt has a positive impact on the world, the process of gathering money for it sometimes involves corporate arm-twisting and departmental quotas, both of which do nothing to build morale. Furthermore, unless specific fund-raising events are planned, contributing to "big business" charity doesn't involve individuals from different groups working together in new and different ways. Thus, it does little or nothing to create a sense of community that transcends organizational barriers.

While Silicon Valley companies are involved in charity work, they aren't nonprofit organizations. They are very serious for-profit companies, with difficult challenges in a highly competitive market. One of the fiercest competitors in the computer industry is Sun Microsystems, a manufacturer of high-powered workstations. According to *Fortune,* Sun is "the most efficient company in the industry," and *Business Week* praised 39-year-old CEO Scott McNealy as "making Sun Microsystems the model for the entire industry, including IBM." He says a big part of Sun's culture is its feeling of community:

> *There's no company I know of that does more hours of volunteer work than this group. It's a community. The communication brings the community. Community has "comm" in it, as does communication. They're really the same words: community and communication. But it's really important to keep focused on the fact that if you don't make money, you lose the pride, you lose the funding, you lose the lifeblood of the organization. We're a community, but we're definitely not a nonprofit organization.*

Corporations Are Communities, Not Machines

How Evolved Is Your Organization?

The following quiz will allow you to assess how far your organization has assimilated, or is free of, the traditional values that a corporation should be like a machine.

The Following Is True . . .

	Always	Frequently	Sometimes	Seldom	Never
1. I often feel like a cog in a gigantic machine.	___	___	___	___	___
2. People here often spend time together after work.	___	___	___	___	___
3. We spend a great deal of time playing with "numbers."	___	___	___	___	___
4. I can send an e-mail to our CEO and not get in trouble.	___	___	___	___	___
5. Reorganizing is a way of life around here.	___	___	___	___	___
6. I feel as if my contribution is truly respected.	___	___	___	___	___
7. My job description is extremely detailed.	___	___	___	___	___
8. I feel like I'm working among my friends.	___	___	___	___	___
9. I often feel as if I am a slave to my computer.	___	___	___	___	___
10. Family members are made wlecome when they visit the workplace.	___	___	___	___	___

Scoring:

For all odd-numbered statements, score:

Always	1
Frequently	2
Sometimes	3
Seldom	4
Never	5

For all even-numbered statements, score:

Always	5
Frequently	4
Sometimes	3
Seldom	2
Never	1

If your score is 10–20: Your organization tends to dehumanize people and to treat them as if they were components rather than individuals. People use rules and regulations to suppress conflict, which sometimes bubbles over into rage. Many people would leave the organization if given an opportunity elsewhere.

If your score is 21–35: Your organization is average. People feel reasonably connected to the organization and know that their contributions matter. Bureaucracy remains a major problem, and it often takes a lot of extra effort to get a job done. Much time is wasted worrying about procedures and policies.

If your score is 36–50: Your organization is close to the Silicon Valley ideal. People feel closely connected to the organization and feel that their personal goals mesh with the organization's goals. People are respected as individuals rather than because of their job titles.

Points to Ponder

In order to create leverage for change, write out the answers to the following questions:

- What could you do to promote a greater level of connection between your organization's leadership and the people who are actually making products, providing services, or serving customers?

  _____

  _____

  _____

  _____

  _____

- What could you do to promote a greater level of connection between your organization's leadership and the people who are actually making products, providing services, or serving customers?

  _____

  _____

  _____

  _____

  _____

- What could you do today to promote a deeper level of electronic communications in your organization?

  _____

  _____

  _____

  _____

  _____

- What would it take to start an in-house day care center or preschool at your corporation and what kind of priorities would the management have to adopt in order to make this a reality?

_____

_____

_____

_____

_____

An organization can't become much of a community if the managers are determined to act like dictators. In order to make the community function correctly, managers have to give up the notion that they're supposed to be bosses. Instead, they must master the third key to Silicon Valley culture . . .

Key No. 3

···

MANAGEMENT IS SERVICE, NOT CONTROL

···

The Silicon Valley Mindset:
Management = Service

Who isn't familiar with Bill Gates, the wunderkind who co-founded Microsoft and today is the richest man in the world? Bill is often in the news, and nearly every action that he and his company take is dissected in the business press. One of the reasons that Bill remains so fascinating is that he's very different from the CEOs of the past. For example, he's often seen wearing the sneakers and sport coats that engineers tend to favor, even though his wealth could obviously purchase Armani suits. But it isn't Bill's appearance that makes him such an interesting character. It's the way that he fills the role of Chairman at Microsoft.

As already noted, most CEOs think of themselves as "running" their companies. They consider themselves "captains of industry" with minions at their beck and call. Not so Bill. The last thing that Bill wants to do is to tell employees exactly what to do. He has no need to control the behavior of his employees; instead he wants to provide them an environment where they can accomplish their and the company's goals. Here's what Bill told me about his role at Microsoft:

At Microsoft, the role of management is to spot emerging trends and set the future direction of the company. The most important and exciting part of my work as Chairman is recognizing what we call "sea changes," and articulating the opportunities they present to each person in the company. We then empower employees with as much information and as many productivity tools as possible, so they can achieve results within the framework of that vision. The hardest part is knowing how to allocate the right resources— bet the store when we must—to make sure it all happens.

Bill is providing a service for the rest of Microsoft. It's his goal to *lead* Microsoft, rather than *run* Microsoft.

Most effective high-tech leaders tend to be as service-oriented as Bill Gates. For example, I asked Edward Mc-Cracken, CEO of Silicon Graphics, how his company has continued to achieve success in such a highly competitive market. He told me that the key to innovation at Silicon Graphics is a lack of formal structure:

The good companies in the computer industry have horizontal organizations; they aren't as hierarchical, and people develop informal project teams with people on the Net. Communications are much easier, and more people know what's going on. And that's important, because if you're going to make quick decisions and get on with things that are changing so fast, you want each individual to be able to make informed decisions. We thrive on self-motivation.

McCracken manages SGI by giving self-motivated individuals the power to make their own decisions. As a result, there's a lot of freedom as SGI and not much bureaucracy. Although SGI, with over 5,000 people, is more than large enough by Industrial Age standards to justify a fairly extensive bureaucracy, it has never developed a significant bureaucracy. Instead, like most other Silicon Valley companies, it has developed a different way of thinking about the process of management. Rather than focusing on controlling employee behavior, high-tech managers try to eliminate control mechanisms and disperse power throughout the organization.

To leaders like Bill Gates, management isn't about control at all; it's about service. This is a difficult concept for many to grasp. We're used to thinking about managers, especially top executives, as people who tell other people what to do. Another reason that the Management = Service mindset seems so foreign is that historically, service has been associated with low-paying, often subservient, jobs. When we hear about the growth of the service economy, we tend to think of people flipping burgers or providing maid service. The notion that a multibillionaire such as Bill Gates provides a service to his own company initially sounds backward.

Effective high-tech leaders encourage and inspire; they help people to envision what the organization and they as individuals are capable of achieving. They also arbitrate when employees can't come to a decision on their own. On rare occasions, they will intervene and reverse decisions when they feel the organization, for one reason or another, goes off course. This, however, is the exception and not the rule. Effective high-tech leaders would rather that their organizations run smoothly and profitably without much management attention. Often, truly effective high-tech leaders view having to intervene in day-to-day decision making as a failure on their part. This is a different attitude from that of the typical corporation, where management meddling is often ubiquitous.

The Traditional Mindset: Management = Control

The idea that the role of management is to control employee behavior emerges naturally from the Business = Battlefield and Corporation = Machine mindsets. Managers who have internalized those two mindsets naturally conclude that they should be in "command" of the troops, and "controlling" the machine.

A major problem with the Management = Control mindset is that it leads corporations to concentrate power at the top. It causes the proliferation of complicated rules and regulations, the growth of bureaucracies, and the need for expensive reporting mechanisms to pass information up and down the management chain. Traditional companies believe that the result of such techniques will be a stronger, in-control corporation. Unfortunately, the actual result is likely to be a brittle and rigid monolith.

One victim of this mindset was Wang Laboratories in the 1980s. Wang was the leading vendor of stand-alone word processors, the special-purpose computers that assistants used to type memos for their bosses. By the mid-1980s, it was pretty clear that low-cost personal computers would replace Wang's pricey word processors as the platform of choice for word processing. This represented a wonderful opportunity for Wang Laboratories, because the software on Wang's word processors was the best and most sophisticated in the world. All Wang had to do was to convert its own word processing software to run on the personal computer, and it would probably have captured the soon-to-be-lucrative market for PC-based word processing software.

Wang didn't do this, however. The management knew that once Wang's leading-edge word processing software was on the personal computer, few people would be willing to buy Wang's word processor units. What Wang failed to realize was that it was only a matter of time before somebody else came up with a workable word processing program for the personal computer. When that happened, Wang's profitability quickly declined.

Wang's decision not to make the transition into PC-based word processing was a direct result of the company's culture, according to a former Wang executive:

> *The organizational structure was extremely rigid. There were seven levels of management between the average product manager and CEO Wang. It's no wonder that he lost track of what was going on inside the company. By 1986, it was clear that personal computers would have a big impact on computing. Despite this, companies like Wang had great difficulty assimilating that fact.*

Wang's problem was that the mechanisms of command and control, rather than making the company stronger, merely made it awkward and unwieldy. The Management = Control mindset can also create a supercharged political atmosphere that saps the energy of the corporation with turf battles, labor unrest, power plays, and all the other futile behaviors that do absolutely nothing to serve customers. The result is often a state of "control gridlock" where even the most basic of tasks—like bringing a product to market—becomes an extraordinarily complicated process involving many signatures, multiple approvals and agreements, and political gyrations.

A good example of this problem is Xerox, a company that's had a great deal of trouble getting products out the door. Here's what a former employee told me about working in a marketing group at Xerox:

> *It was incredible. Everything, from the press release to the product description to the information sheet had to be reviewed and approved by multiple vice presidents and announcement committees. We spent almost six months trudging through the paperwork. If one committee or VP made a change to a paragraph, the other committees and VPs had to approve it. Even with electronic mail, it was an unbelievable hassle. Everything had to comply*

with corporate standards, even though some of the standards were inconsistent and often out-of-date. What was sad about the situation is that all these people sincerely believed that they were helping the company to be successful. There was no conception whatsoever that all this folderol was one of the reasons that Xerox was losing market share. They didn't have a clue.

We've been told for so many years that managers are supposed to be in charge that any other definition of management seems absurd or naive. All too often, well-meaning managers try to control their way out of problems, control the behavior of the people who work with them, control events that are going to happen whether they like it or not.

It's a popular business myth that large organizations need more control than smaller ones; in other words, the bigger the company, the bigger the bureaucracy. But even small organizations can be crippled by managers who believe that their position is dependent on trying to control events and employee behavior. Companies like Microsoft and Hewlett-Packard make it abundantly clear that organizations can be large and remain flexible.

One marketing specialist who's worked for a number of high-tech firms, told me a story of when he was hired by an eight-person software start-up company. He had spent the preceding few years at a large company (it was one of the minicomputer vendors) and was relieved to have the chance to work for a small company that presumably would be free of the political infighting and bureaucracy that had made his last job so miserable. When he arrived at his new job, the marketing vice president called him into her office and informed him that she didn't want him to speak directly to the company's president. If he had any comments or complaints, he was to talk to her first. "We've got to maintain discipline and order," she told him. At first the specialist thought that she was joking—after all, there were only eight people in the entire company—but the rigid expression on her face told him that she was deadly serious. Not surprisingly, the company quickly ran into major problems and was nearly forced out of business.

The need to control can be very seductive. The illusion that we can bend other people's hearts and minds and get them to do exactly what we want is a comforting one in a world that's admittedly chaotic. What's most dangerous about "control" is that it works—at least for a while, but it eventually creates massive resentment. The controlling person looks around the conference table one day and finds that he or she is surrounded by enemies—people who would stab the controlling manager in the back, if given half a chance. So the manager comes up with some new way to control or manipulate, while the employees continue to maneuver and posture to avoid the heavy hand of management.

What's the alternative to control? Chaos? That's what best-selling author and management consultant Tom Peters would have us believe. Peters wrote a book, *Thriving on Chaos*, encouraging managers to embrace chaos, to channel it, to make chaos an integral part of the organization. Industry savant and venture capitalist Ann Winblad commented:

> *The software industry as a whole tends to be slightly managed chaos. It was a giant "group grope" in the late 1970s when this whole thing started. Because of the fast growth of new segments, that has not changed. It probably is a little bit more civilized working at a large software company like Oracle than at a start-up down the street, but only marginally. I mean, they might have fancier buildings and a security system and name tags, but effectively, there are no rules.*

Think about that: "Effectively, there are no rules." Inside companies that follow the Silicon Valley management model, the addiction to control has been replaced by a different understanding of what management is all about. Effective managers inside Silicon Valley cultures set the overall direction of the organization and then let the employees decide how they're going to go after those opportunities. This Management = Service mindset results in a very different set of behaviors from the Management = Control mindset, as shown in Table 3.1.

To illustrate how these two mindsets produce different business results, let's look at how Hewlett-Packard overtook Digital Equipment Corporation as the second largest computer company in the United States.

TABLE 3.1
COMPARISON OF CONTROL AND SERVICE MINDSETS

MANAGEMENT = CONTROL

• *Gridlock.* The attempt to control creates resistance and spawns other attempts to control, causing decision making to grind to a halt.

• *Yes Man Syndrome.* People agree with their managers even when there are better ideas and better ways to approach a situation.

• *Limited Power.* Control concentrated at the top limits the exercise of power to the executives, slowing corporate growth.

MANAGEMENT = SERVICE

• *Creative Dissent.* Different opinions and ideas result in a variety of approaches and ways of accomplishing a task.

• *Flexibility.* Important decisions are moved away from top management and closer to the customer, making the company more responsive.

• *Empowerment.* Dispersing control downward increases the amount of power in the organization, making it more viable.

Case Study: The Organizational Structures of Hewlett-Packard and Digital

Hewlett-Packard (HP) is unique among all the computer vendors that were part of the 1970s boom in that it has weathered the vast changes in the past fifteen years without the layoffs, bankruptcies, and market share losses that have crippled many of the rest.

As mentioned earlier, HP was founded in 1939 by Bill Hewlett and Dave Packard, two electrical engineers from Stanford University. They had some unusual ideas about how to lead their fledgling company, which were contrary to management theories of that time. The 1940s and 1950s were a time when management was considered a science, and business schools encouraged managers to run companies "by the numbers." Boiled down to its essence, this meant maximizing profit by paying employees as little as possible to do their jobs. This kind of management remains popular today, according to Rafael Aguayo in his 1990 book *Dr. Deming: The American Who Taught the Japanese about Quality*.

Bill Hewlett and Dave Packard believed that a corporation would be more productive if employees also benefited from the corporation's success. Further, they believed that workers deserved a stable environment, absent of the hire-and-fire turmoil common in the electronics industry of the time. They also considered a strong corporation to be like a community, and created a tradition of informality; from the start, they were "Bill" and "Dave" to their employees. Finally, HP's founders pointed employees in the right direction and let them do their jobs. Micromanagement had no place inside HP's corporate culture. Bill and Dave created a culture in which management was a service to the people doing the work. HP grew and prospered, and increasingly by the late 1970s, HP's revenues were coming from computer products such as the HP 3000 minicomputer.

One of HP's major competitors at this time was Massachusetts-based Digital Equipment Corporation. Digital was founded in 1957 by Ken Olsen, an electrical engineer from MIT. As Digital grew, Ken—a self-styled puritan who neither drank, smoked, or swore—centralized control of the company, purging anybody who represented a possible threat to his authority. This process, documented in Rifkin and Harrar's 1988 book *The Ultimate Entrepreneur: The Story of Ken Olsen and Digital Equipment Corporation*, resulted in a company that ran according to Ken's every whim. He even coined a corporate motto to epitomize his concept of Digital: "One Company, One Strategy, One Message." Ken's motto was symbolic of his determination to be an absolute monarch. It was the Management = Control mindset taken to an extreme. This attitude, and the resulting organizational structure, became a major weakness at Digital, according to Jim Manzi, then CEO of neighboring Lotus Development Corporation:

> *One of the things that killed Digital was the "Ken Says" phenomenon. You know, unless "Ken said," nothing happened. It was a very Copernican world where everything revolved around Ken. That's true in all sorts of companies. But that's death in today's world.*

By 1980, HP and Digital were similar on the surface, both selling minicomputers to the same kind of customers. Beneath the surface, however, things were very different. HP had a decentralized and flexible corporate culture that trusted employees to make decisions on their own. Digital, on the other hand, had a corporate culture that was permeated with control. At that time, Digital was the more successful; in fact, Digital was the world's largest minicomputer vendor and soon to become North America's second largest computer vendor (after IBM). By 1988, Digital was still in the lead, enjoying $12.4 billion in yearly revenues, a little less than twice HP's yearly computer revenues.

By 1994, the positions of the two companies had reversed. HP's yearly sales were up to $24 billion, and the company was growing at a breakneck 24 percent per year. Digital's revenues had stalled at $13.5 billion, less than they were in 1988 when adjusted for inflation. And worse, Digital's growth rate was a depressing 6.4 percent. HP was enjoying record profits, while Digital had recently experienced a series of record losses. Hewlett-Packard's CEO Lew Platt told me how HP accomplished this:

> *Hewlett-Packard is very much managed by culture. A lot of things around here just happen because that is the right way to do things at HP. We are a very decentralized company. We're broken down into relatively small business units. We give people who run the businesses a lot of freedom in terms of making decisions about what they ought to be doing. We don't try to steer everything from the top of the company. I think that gives us the advantages of being big—and there are some—while it allows us to avoid most of the disadvantages.*

According to Lew, being decentralized has kept HP closer to its customers. Because decisions are made closer to the customer, HP makes products that customers want. He believes that HP's decentralization is responsible for HP avoiding the arrogance and complacency that developed at IBM and Digital. He explained:

> *You can't start believing that you're invincible or that you know what customers want more than they do. That has been the Achilles' heel of many companies in this industry, particularly our*

two biggest competitors. They became complacent. And, when they became complacent, they decided that they knew what customers needed better than the customers knew. They stopped listening, and they started missing all the subtle signals in the marketplace that they would have picked up had they been more alert.

Decentralization helped HP to remain responsive to customer requirements. As a result, HP entered the personal computer market early. Today, HP's widely dispersed and decentralized divisions not only sell desktop computers, they produce a line of portable and ultrasmall computers. HP's printer division virtually dominates the market for desktop printers. And HP is one of the most innovative companies in the computer industry, leading the research and development for new technologies such as the superfast P7 microprocessor that HP and Intel are building together.

HP has successfully adapted to the new computer industry because its decentralized structure made it possible to create innovative products quickly. Not that it's been easy. The computer industry of the 1990s has changed radically from the computer industry of the 1970s. Like the other traditional computer vendors in the 1990s, HP has had to deal with lower margins, fiercer competition, and an ever-more-demanding customer base. What's interesting is the way that HP reacted to these major challenges. Rather than trying to consolidate control at the top as many companies would have done, HP reacted by decentralizing even further. CEO Lew Platt explained:

If you study carefully the history of HP, you will find in every case—and I am more certain about this than anything else I've said to you today—when we've gotten into trouble, it has always—not almost always—it has always been followed by a period of decentralization and pushing decision making down. That's just the way we respond. And, again, it works. And because it works and because HP people tend to be around for a very long time, there are always a lot of people who remember the last time that it worked. Therefore, you have a large number of people who are willing to bet that it will work again. There's a quote that I particularly like: "The role of the CEO is to make the invisible visible and to manage the white spaces." That is a clever way of saying that the CEO is really responsible for the sense of connectedness within the company, the white spaces being those things between the functions or the businesses on the organization chart. I really like that definition of the CEO's job. I think that's what the CEO's job is all about, and I spend a lot of my time doing it.

By contrast, Digital's top-heavy structure made if difficult for the company to launch the products that customers wanted. Founder Ken Olsen didn't like personal computers and didn't see why people needed them. This prejudice was widespread at Digital's corporate headquarters, which held most of Digital's decision-making power. As a result, Digital didn't launch a viable personal computer business until ten years after the IBM PC had been released.

Unlike HP, which decentralized further in response to financial problems, Digital, consistent with its Management = Control culture, increased the level of control when Digital's financial fortunes began to wane. Digital's management instituted top-down financial controls and strengthened the power of the internal bureaucracy. The board of directors hired "strong" managers from traditional companies such as IBM, hoping that they could "pull the company together." Then the layoffs started. In the first rounds, most of the people who were laid off were "in the field," far away from corporate headquarters. In essence, Digital purged the very people who were closest to the customers and might have been able to help Digital adapt to changing customer requirements.

Implementation Strategies

I recently attended a meeting of 20 chief information officers (CIOs) at which the subject of cross-functional teams was discussed in some detail. The CIOs who worked in traditional organizations were highly skeptical of the value of teams. "We tried them, but they didn't work," was the most common comment. Traditional organizations often have enormous difficulty implementing decentralized organizations because their cultural mindsets don't provide the infrastructure for the strategy. The influence of culture on organizational strategy is shown in Figure 3.1.

However, when the Management = Service mindset has been thoroughly assimilated inside an organization, it becomes possible to execute three successful strategies that make organizations far more responsive and adaptable:

- *Increase power by dispersing it.*
- *Encourage creative dissent.*
- *Build autonomous teams.*

Let's examine each of these strategies.

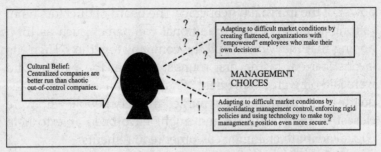

FIGURE 3.1   *Culture Limits Management Choices*

STRATEGY 7: INCREASE POWER BY DISPERSING IT

Traditional companies concentrate control at the top of the company through the formation of a powerful bureaucracy at corporate headquarters. At many companies, that bureaucracy can become, like government bureaucracy, an impediment to meaningful change.

Masayoshi Son is the CEO of SOFTBANK, the world's largest publisher of computer-related magazines and books and the world's largest producer of technology-related trade shows. Masayoshi is clear about the ever-present dangers of bureaucracy:

Whatever the country, whatever the culture, whatever the time, when you become a big enough organization, you start to collapse and slow down. Then the bureaucracy builds up, creating all kinds of friction, and the growth of the company slows down. The flatter you can make your organization, the less you have to worry about bureaucracy.

Effective high-tech leaders make a constant effort to avoid the bureaucratic encrustations that plague so many other companies. Hewlett-Packard CEO Lew Platt commented:

I am convinced that bureaucracy and centralization tend to accumulate over time. I'm fond of drawing a parallel to what happens in your garage. Junk accumulates, and if you don't clean house periodically, you find you can't park your car! Bureaucracy is the same way. It's always creeping into the system, and periodically you have to stand back and really clean it out. We do that. We're reasonably good at doing that. We've taken things such as our corporate headquarters' functions and have an annual review of them. The businesses get to vote on whether they want them to continue. That helps us clean out whatever bureaucracy has crept in.

At HP, you have a perfect example of the Industrial Age corporation set on its ear. In most companies, the various divisions have to go to corporate bureaucracies every year, begging for approval to continue their work. At HP, the situation is exactly reversed; the corporate functions have to go to the divisions for funding.

This means redefining the role of management so that control is less important than coordination. Y.S. Kim, former head of Samsung's Korean PC business and CEO of California-based AST Research, explains:

> *The CEO's job is to orchestrate individual accomplishment so that their sum is much greater than it otherwise would be. I expect my staff to report to me what they've done rather than ask me what to do. Each employee has to decide what to do, because the employee knows best. If you don't empower people, the organization can't grow.*

Effective high-tech leaders also keep power from accumulating at the top of the organization by making sure that they, as CEOs, don't cling to a need to tell people what to do. One CEO who has become a master of this is Mitchell Kertzman. I asked him the secret to becoming an effective manager. Here's what he told me:

> *I am the reverse of the Peter Principle. When I started the company, it was a one-man business. There was a time when I did every job in this company. I wrote the programs, I sent out the bills, I did the accounting, I answered the phone, I made the coffee. As the company has grown, I do fewer and fewer of those jobs. And that's just as well, because I was certainly less competent at them than most of the people who are doing them now. I'm the reverse of the Peter Principle in the sense that I've finally risen to my level of competence, which is that I don't do anything very well and now what I do extremely well is nothing. Now,*

what am I good at? I'm good at motivation. I'm good at recruiting. I'm good at representing the company. I'm good at giving speeches. I'm good at meeting with customers, meeting with the press, working with the financial community. So, my job has become what I'm good at.

For Mitchell, the process of growth as a manager was the process of giving up control, responsibility, and authority. The key to personal growth as a manager is to recognize your weaknesses and then overcome them by hiring great team members. Giving up control is different from delegating, according to Mitchell. As he explained it, managers who delegate are still tied up in the need to control:

The unwillingness to let go is almost a pathology. They know—intellectually—that they need to hire good people to do these things, but then they don't let go. Part of the problem is delegating. Delegating implies that the job is yours but you are delegating it to someone else to do in your place. That's different from saying, "I'm the CEO and the whole company's performance is my responsibility, but running operations belongs to Joe, and running finance belongs to Jane." It's my job to encourage them, provide them the resources that they need, support them, be critical.

There's a definite "service" orientation to Mitchell's view of management. That doesn't mean that he lacks power. Because he's so respected, people listen to what he has to say, and ultimately, the decision-making power rests with him. However, to increase the overall power in the organization, he's chosen to disperse it, using it himself only rarely.

Management = Control also contributes to weak corporate structures by insisting that managers can, and should, know everything that's going on inside an organization. This is a big mistake, according to former Lotus CEO Jim Manzi:

Hierarchy and authority exist in people's minds and perspectives. My greatest fear is having people walk around this company saying, "Jim says we should do this" or "Jim says we do that." The truth is that Jim really doesn't know what these people are talking about because there is a ton of stuff going on in the company. My goal is to make sure that everybody's working in a common direction. I tell people that I don't know what they're talking about. I tell them to leave me out of it. I tell them this is not something I get involved in. I'm very explicit. I'm trying not to encourage the notion that I know everything that's going on in the company, which is a disease a lot of managers have.

In other words, truly effective high-tech managers relinquish control to make the entire organization more powerful. Frank Ingari, CEO of Shiva, commented on this seeming paradox:

Let me ask you something: Do you think power is finite, or do you think power is a renewable resource and, in fact, a global resource inside the company? What happens in the large company is that sooner or later people begin to believe that power and all the associated goodies—power for its own sake, power as an aphrodisiac, power as access to money, power as access to bosses—is a finite pool. For one person to have power, another has to lose it. Despite what people think, that's not true, even in a large company. In fact, it's a sign of impending death when people inside a company start believing that. Nothing could be further from the truth. Power doesn't derive from what happens inside these four walls. Power derives from our effect in the marketplace, and from what we're able to generate within ourselves in terms of creative activity. Therefore, by definition, the exact opposite is true. Power can and must be grown. The successful company is growing its power.

Therein lies the real meaning of the much-abused word *empowerment*—by giving up control, by empowering people in the organization, you make it more robust, more adaptable, more flexible, and, therefore, more powerful. Here's how AST Research CEO Y.S. Kim put it:

> *Employees have to be given more individual responsibility in order to perform at their best. Loyalty comes from having pride in what we do. This means giving people more responsibility in the decision making process, widening the so-called "span of control" so that more people are executing more tasks. This creates a driving imperative in terms of reward and recognition.*

STRATEGY 8: ENCOURAGE CREATIVE DISSENT

Dispersing power into an organization won't work if managers, including CEOs, get into a huff every time somebody in the organization does something that management doesn't like. Managers can't constantly be intervening to make things the way they want it. This means they must tolerate and encourage dissent, even if that dissent is with the management itself. This strategy is illustrated by the following story that Mitchell Kertzman told me about the way he manages:

> *A while back, a junior manager in the company came up with an idea that I thought was really dumb. And I made it very clear that I thought it was dumb. He went ahead and did it anyway. Well, I was wrong and he turned out to be exactly right. The important part, culturally, is that I should be able to stand up and acknowledge that I was wrong, and support a person who, in spite of my disagreement, went ahead and did what turned out to be the right thing.*

Mitchell let the junior manager do what he thought was appropriate and Mitchell was willing to admit that he was wrong. This kind of event rarely, if ever, happens in a company with a traditional business culture because that junior manager would never have dared to disagree with his traditional CEO in the first place. And he undoubtedly would have been fired had he taken an action that was contrary to the CEO's opinions about the right way to do things, regardless of whether it worked or not.

This calls for a more sensitive style of management, one that builds upon trust. Stan Shih, CEO of Acer Group, explains:

> In the past, control is controlled by who owns 51 percent of the company. It makes much more sense to control a company by managing the common interest of the people inside of it. This kind of approach, however, takes longer to establish because you have to establish a consensus, which requires a lot of communication and mutual trust. And then we can share the common vision and common goal and reach strategies that serve the mutual benefit.

Inside Silicon Valley-style companies, the process of decision making is collaborative, with the manager playing a role as arbitrator, coach, and mentor rather than officer, owner, and dictator. This isn't to say that the high-tech leaders can't or won't make decisions. They do make final decisions, but generally only when employees can't come to agreement.

William Campbell, the CEO of Intuit, the company that makes the most popular personal finance software in the world believes that controlling organizations strip away individual initiative. Employees metamorphose into "yes men" and corporate "fraidy cats," a problem he saw at IBM:

> IBM is like the Stepford Wives. It takes the best people from the best colleges and universities in the country and then snips out some part of the brain so that they become mindless clones. They're still, individually, some of the smartest people I know, and I really enjoy them when I get them in a bar. But inside of IBM, they don't

protest, they don't fight anything, they're afraid to take risks.
They're always talking about what won't fly in the company.

In his leadership role, Bill tries to set up a corporate environment where there's plenty of controversy, opinions, and conflict. He uses this as a way to get people involved in the decision-making process:

You get used to working with equals. It makes you manage differently. The hierarchical manager of yesterday ran the Industrial Age company with "Yes sir! Yes sir! Anything you want, sir! I'm right with you sir!" Now it's all different. People talking to management say things like, "Bill, that's bullshit. That's stupid. You made a dumb decision." That's the difference. When you're running an Information Age company, you've got to allow a lot of dissent. In fact, you have to foster dissent. One of my principles is that if I can't defend it, I shouldn't be doing it. What point is there in mindless agreement? I won't accept "Yes Sir!" for an answer. When you're working in these companies, you're with people who are older than you, younger than you, smarter than you. You have to remember that the board made you the boss, but your people make you the leader.

As you might imagine, debates have often become spirited inside the companies that Bill's managed. But that's par for the course at companies that manage the Silicon Valley way. When managers yell, employees yell right back at them. Bill Campbell commented on this:

I like people to fight back, and I hate people who just say "yes." I've got a temper, you know. I'm angry a lot—not abusive. But when I'm in your face, I expect you to come back at me with "Shit, Bill, I looked at it that way. It didn't work that way." That is ultimate management, in my view. I want people who aren't afraid to tell me what the hell's going on. You've got to be able to talk about it. I want you to hear me, and I want me to hear you. We're all interested in that one goal, the ultimate goal—making this company better.

Organizations with Silicon Valley cultures create a work atmosphere in which issues can be discussed openly, without undue concern about treading on toes or violating turf. In a truly effective organization, people generally aren't respected because of *position* but because of *contribution*. According to a 1994 article in *Wired* magazine, a hot programmer at Microsoft may have far more clout than an executive. This creates a true meritocracy, where a higher level of contribution creates a higher level of influence. Mitchell Kertzman, CEO of Sybase, pointed out:

> *You need a culture where (a) it's possible to put any crackpot idea on the table, (b) it's appropriate to say it's a crackpot idea, but (c) that can never translate into a negative comment on the individual who put it on the table. So, people must have the courage to put things on the table and the courage to take the criticism when it comes. But, that's the kind of environment we have. It's a demanding, stimulating, tough environment. We had a management meeting recently when we discussed this very issue. There were some expressions of concern that maybe we were too tough on some people and some ideas. We talked it through and decided that this should remain a place where ideas get thrown into the cauldron and get mixed around. What always seems to come out of that process—painful though it may be—is great strategies, great products, and great ideas.*

STRATEGY 9: BUILD AUTONOMOUS TEAMS

Dispersing power throughout an organization requires more than just encouraging dissent. It requires an organizational vehicle that can absorb and utilize power. Microsoft has a culture that does just that. Bill Gates remains a pervasive influence, but much decision making is done by employee teams, according to former Microsoft executive vice president Mike Maples:

We organize into small teams. We have clear goals and objectives and missions for each team, and then we consciously don't have anyone watching them. There's nobody to report when they're not doing what they said they'd do—other than themselves. Part of the secret is behaving like you're small, allowing the teams to behave as if they're independent, as if they're small businesses themselves. They make many of their own decisions. Our development process doesn't require them to get signoff along the way.

At Microsoft, teams generally have near-total responsibility for their success or failure. They're expected to do whatever it takes to make their product successful, without meddling advice from corporate headquarters. Mike Maples continued:

If Bill [Gates] or I or some of the other senior managers want to review where the teams are, we can ask to do so, but the teams never have to wait until they've been reviewed. If we don't get involved, they just go from start to finish by themselves. We've tried to create an environment where people are responsible to themselves for their success. If you're clear on what their goals and objectives are at the beginning, and they understand what they're trying to accomplish and you understand what they're trying to accomplish, it works pretty well.

Successful companies in Silicon Valley and elsewhere have found that small, autonomous teams are more likely to be responsive to customer needs. Small teams, too, are far less likely to develop the kind of inertia that keeps big organizations from adapting to changes in the market. Former Novell CEO Bob Frankenberg commented on this:

> *We have small teams that are going to be able to move product out the door without having to change everything else in the product. But the most important thing is to be able to get people who understand a set of needs better than anyone else in the world in a particular area, and then let them move to address that need. If you don't have the connection to the customer or the ability to handle the enormous amount of information that's involved, then you end up with a monolithic structure.*

Organizing into small teams enables them to function like small businesses. Each team has the necessary talent to make the product and the team successful. This frees the team to focus on what's important—the success of the product in terms of its ability to satisfy customer needs. Under these conditions, organizational politics become less important. Rather than kowtowing to review committees and turf protecting nabobs, the team can do whatever it takes to make its product a winner.

Small teams also increase the responsiveness of an organization, according to Masayoshi Son, CEO of SOFTBANK:

> *At SOFTBANK, each team consists of less than ten people and each has its own balance sheet. This arrangement makes it easier to motivate people by making them feel important enough to have an impact on a bottom line. Building small teams lets them have the "feel" of the business both directly and dynamically. In a very very real way, it helps the entire company to remain more sensitive to the marketplace.*

The same is true at HCL, according to Chairman Shiv Nadar:

> *We built our company by making smaller units led by chief executives who have an entrepreneurial flair. We let them build their own organizations with their own staff and their own management groups. The fewer layers of management, the better.*

Giving up the notion of management control is particularly important for organizations that are dispersed around the world. Acer Group CEO Stan Shih puts it this way:

> *When globalizing, you always have limited resources of talent and capital. The best way to globalize is therefore to localize, to integrate the local resources of talent and capital and integrate it with the parent company. We think in terms of "global brand, local touch," and try to form a group that leverages the size of the parent company but still draws on the experience of the local partners. You must have a common vision and a goal, but implementation must be based upon the local leaders' management style.*

The idea that Management = Service allows companies to give teams the autonomy that they need to get the job done. Leaders don't try to second-guess or review everything that their employees do. Hewlett-Packard CEO Lew Platt comments:

> *In organizations that have very tight controls, you usually find that the top management is prescribing how things will be done because there isn't the trust of individuals that makes it possible to give them freedom. [HP founders] Dave and Bill always emphasized that, as a manager, I work on what needs to be accomplished and leave it up to the individuals to figure out how to accomplish it. That's management by objectives, long before it was even called that. Again, it works well in an organization where you have enough confidence in the culture that it will put boundary conditions around the way people do things.*

Success Secrets from Silicon Valley

How Evolved Is Your Organization?

The following quiz will allow you to assess how far your management has assimilated, or is free of, the destructive notion that their job is to tell people what to do:

··

The Following Is True . . .

	Always	Frequently	Sometimes	Seldom	Never
1. A person could get fired for disobeying a foolish order.	___	___	___	___	___
2. Managers take the time to help people to learn.	___	___	___	___	___
3. The managers have much nicer offices than workers.	___	___	___	___	___
4. I can count on my manager to get me the resources I need.	___	___	___	___	___
5. Even unimportant decisions must be manager-approved.	___	___	___	___	___
6. I feel as if I have more power than my peers in other firms.	___	___	___	___	___
7. Nobody argues with the boss around here.	___	___	___	___	___
8. My manager respects people who have different opinions.	___	___	___	___	___
9. We have teams, but they don't have any real power.	___	___	___	___	___
10. Electronic mail flattens our management chain.	___	___	___	___	___

··

Scoring:

For all odd-numbered statements, score:

Always	1
Frequently	2
Sometimes	3
Seldom	4
Never	5

For all even-numbered statements, score:

Always	5
Frequently	4
Sometimes	3
Seldom	2
Never	1

If your score is 10–20: Your management has a highly traditional notion of their role inside the organization. Managers give very detailed instructions, which they expect to be followed exactly. Decisions are often arbitrary and made without discussion.

If your score is 21–35: Your organization is average. Decision-making often takes a great deal of time, due to the complexities of running things up and down the management chain. Some managers are better than others at getting people involved.

If your score is 36–50: Your organization is close to the Silicon Valley ideal. Decisions are made quickly, and at the appropriate level inside the company. Managers allow teams to make their own decisions and usually intervene only when the team can't decide on its own.

Points to Ponder

In order to create leverage for change, write out the answers to the following questions:

• When you need to get things done, do you try to manipulate people to get what you want or do you encourage them to deal with the problem as they see fit?

_____

_____

_____

_____

_____

• What do you think is the inner motivation and maturity level of a manager who needs the constant obedience of those who surround him (or her)?

_____

_____

_____

_____

_____

• What would have to happen for the teams in your organization to be able to make decisions on their own, without management interference?

_____

_____

_____

_____

_____

• What would the managers and employees in your company have to believe about themselves to make bureaucracy a thing of the past?

_____

_____

_____

_____

_____

If managers are to give up the notion that they should be giving orders, along with our notions of management, our notions about the nature of employment must change as well. That's the reasoning behind the fourth key to Silicon Valley culture . . .

Key No. 4

....

EMPLOYEES ARE PEERS,
NOT CHILDREN

....

The Silicon Valley Mindset:
Employees = Peers

Earlier, we talked about how the employees of Silicon Valley companies work hard not only because they need to get their work done, but because they feel they're part of a community. We also talked about how managers inside Silicon Valley business cultures set up autonomous teams, a strategy that puts decision making where it belongs—closer to the customer. As noted, these concepts are put into practice under the umbrella of the Business = Ecosystem mindset, which encourages people to value cooperation over conflict and diversity over uniformity.

Also motivating the productivity and dedication of the employee is the knowledge that he or she is regarded as a peer. A word heard frequently in Silicon Valley is *meritocracy*. Meritocracy is a system in which people are judged based on their achievements and contributions to an organization. A fancy title on a business card is not what determines someone's professional value.

The idea of a meritocracy also includes the notion that a person with merit is somebody who contributes to the best of his or her ability. This means that a truly excellent janitor is as deserving of respect as a truly excellent vice president. Frank Ingari, CEO of Shiva, explained:

In my opinion, if a job deserves to be done, then it deserves the equivalent respect of any other job. That's a core value. And I think that this applies not only in work, but in personal life. Let's say you've got a relative who is a truck driver. Well, why is he a truck driver? Is he good at it? Does he enjoy himself? Does he give time to his kids? Don't judge a person based on these arbitrary notions of how someone chooses his or her trajectory in life or what he or she happens to have been given genetically. I'm not trying to give you an egalitarian message. All I'm trying to say is make sure you don't value people according to arbitrary society values, because that's all ephemeral.

The concept of Employee = Peer promotes the notion that nobody is inherently superior to anybody else; therefore no one person should be ordering everyone else around. Hence, our truly excellent and respected janitor doesn't need to be constantly watched or supervised, because it's assumed that he or she is self-motivated enough to do the job well. That also means that you can afford to pay the janitor more because it reduces the need for a supervisor to look over the janitor's shoulder.

In addition to promoting respect between employees, the Employee = Peer mindset strengthens teamwork. When employees are assumed to be fundamentally equal, an employee may be a leader one day, and a follower the next. This makes it easier to form teams to accomplish short-term tasks, without posturing over who's top dog. When an employee is a peer, that employee will tend to strive for personal excellence and still take the time to help other employees achieve their goals. Employees with this level of confidence then are comfortable vying for the most difficult projects, setting ambitious deadlines, and basking in their teams' successes.

This is a very different approach from that currently in many companies, where managers try to control employee behavior. In traditional companies, it's common for managers to treat employees either as if they are children who have to be watched all the time. And what's particularly dangerous about the Employee = Child mindset is that it can become a self-fulfilling prophecy.

The Traditional Mindset: Employee = Child

The labor practices that developed from Employee = Child mindset originated in Europe during the early years of the Industrial Revolution and were defined by a strict class system. Factory owners were aristocrats who were regarded by themselves and by society as superior to the laborers they hired. Just as landed gentry had instituted serfdom, factory owners saw laborers as tools with which to produce their goods. The more "kindly" factory owners treated laborers as children, who needed to be guided and disciplined. In fact, in many factories at that time, a majority of the laborers *were* children. By the time child labor was outlawed, the die was cast: employees were treated as if they still were immature, somehow "lesser" beings.

This attitude neatly dovetails with the Business = Battlefield mindset. Throughout history, armies have recruited primarily from the young, who are more impressionable and easily molded. It further connects to and reinforces the Management = Control belief.

Trust is at issue here, too. Traditionally, companies define complicated rules, procedures, and guidelines to govern nearly every aspect of working life. These rules suggest to employees that they are not trustworthy, lack common sense, and have even less capacity for making important decisions. This is what creates micromanagement. Employees who "break the rules" or "misbehave" are considered insubordinate and must be disciplined, like disobedient children.

Let us not forget that employees are people who drive cars, have sex, vote, have children of their own, and manage to lead their lives without the benefit of a corporate "parent." Paternalistic corporate behaviors go largely unexamined, however, because the Employee = Child mindset is so ingrained into the dominant corporate culture.

As mentioned, the infantilization of the workforce can become a self-fulfilling prophecy. Put simply, when you treat people like children, they act like children. Disgruntled from the absence of trust and disgusted with management's patronizing attitude, employees unintentionally become participants in a corporate culture where it's tempting to waste money, waste time, or even steal company property. Frank Ingari, CEO of Shiva, commented on this phenomenon:

One of my first jobs outside of my father's company was with Western Electric. It was fascinating. We went to the office in the morning and got our assignments for the day from a computer. I was a cable monkey and, every day, they'd give us all the cables we were going to lay that day and how many minutes it would take us to do the job, all of which would add up to eight hours worth of work. When we finished that work, we were done for the day. Well, you can imagine, these cable guys weren't stupid. They never, ever, finished a job early. People were "disconnected" from the company. Nobody regarded the phone company as "our" company. That was the farthest thing from our minds. There was no distinction between the phone company, the post office, or IBM. The phone company was a bunch of WASP guys who pulled up in their Cadillacs and bland governmental stuff that we didn't understand. That feeling of disconnection results in the worst kind of sabotage. It's worse than theft. It's just not giving a shit. The only time you care is when you're being watched—if then.

The situation becomes cyclical. Soon, not only is management treating employees like children, but the employees are acting like children. Managers and employees become trapped in a dysfunctional relationship that makes high levels of productivity virtually impossible.

And it isn't just manual laborers who are treated this way. White collar employees, too, in many companies are suspected of stealing office supplies, so management locks the supply cabinets, forcing employees to fill out a form to get a pen or printer cartridge. The absence of trust is implicit. And locking up office supplies forces people to spend valuable work time just accessing the tools they need to do their jobs. This is seen as necessary, however, otherwise employees (children) will be dipping into the corporate cookie jar. I know two Fortune 100 companies whose top management issued companywide memoranda complaining about the overuse of paper clips! Try to imagine, in the real world, a conversation between two adults where one suggests that the other should use fewer paper clips. This is pettiness taken to an almost insane extreme.

Another way managers insult employees is to reward themselves, even while expecting employees to implement cost-savings. For example, I worked for a company that had gotten itself into financial difficulties and consequently initiated a series of draconian cost controls. The president of the company delivered a speech via companywide closed-circuit television, which we listened to in a wired-up conference room. After making a few remarks about company loyalty and the importance of saving money, the president announced that he was accepting a substantial pay raise. A stunned silence filled the room. People started gathering up their notebooks and leaving the room before the broadcast was over. What was fascinating was that the president had no idea that he was giving a double message. Whatever incentive his employees might have had to save money was totally lost.

Having a culture that embraces the "Employee = Child" mindset creates an organization that can't utilize the experience and capabilities of the people inside it. To illustrate this, let's look at how two very different computer companies tried to enter the U.S. computer market.

Case Study: Groupe Bull and Acer
Enter the U.S. Computer Market

Four out of every ten PCs are bought in the United States, according to International Data Corporation—over 26 million units a year. That's four times the number sold in Japan and twice the number sold in all of Asia. It's in the United States that new technology gets adopted first, driving the rest of the computer industry. Computer manufacturers outside of the United States have long understood that in order to remain viable outside of the United States, they must be able to compete inside as well. That hasn't proven easy, however. For example, in the mid 1980s, Groupe Bull purchased the ailing Honeywell Information Systems in a clear attempt to break into the U.S. computer market. Unfortunately, Groupe Bull did this in a way that was profoundly disrespectful of the employees in the acquired company.

The first action of the new top management was to rename the company "Bull Worldwide Information Systems." American employees hated the new name, because in the United States the term "Bull" is shorthand for the final product of a bull's digestive process as well as slang for an outlandish falsehood. When the U.S.-based employees tried to explain this to the new management, they were ignored, much as one ignores a child who complains about something that seems irrelevant to its parent.

The top management stubbornly clung to the "Bull" name, creating havoc among the salesforce. As one salesman put it, "Whenever I make a sales call, the customer just starts laughing." Because it didn't respect the inputs from its employees, the company entered the market with a corporate image that was driving away business.

But that was just the tip of the iceberg. Groupe Bull's idea for the United States market was to sell French-built hardware and software into the U.S. market, even though it was obsolete. When the U.S.-based employees pointed this out, they were ignored, with the clear implication was that top management knew best. At the same time, Groupe Bull began pulling the plug on U.S.-based development efforts that might have produced newer and more competitive products. It was a classic case of top-down management, combined with the belief that the employees were like children—unable to make decisions about what would sell in their own territory. Predictably, Groupe Bull's venture failed and the company's U.S. revenues have been completely dwarfed by companies like Compaq and Dell, which were mere start-ups when Groupe Bull first tried to enter the United States market.

Contrast Groupe Bull's approach with the way that Taiwan-based Acer entered the U.S. PC market. In 1995 and 1996, the fastest growing computer manufacturer in the world was the Acer Group, headquartered in Taiwan. Unlike the satraps at Groupe Bull, Founder and Chairman Stan Shih makes no effort to centralize corporate control. Instead, Acer works with local investors in each geography to set up a subsidiary that has significant local ownership and investment. Local ownership allows Acer to expand manufacturing capacity and market share using less of Acer's own capital. This is a perfect application of the Silicon Valley strategy of "increasing power by dispersing it."

According to the Stan Shih, the CEO of the parent company, Acer's goal is to become twenty-one separately traded companies. Stan feels that Acer can become stronger and more flexible if there is significant local ownership of its subsidiaries than if Acer tried to control the company from the top down. As a result, local subsidiaries can make decisions about the needs of their market without kowtowing to Taipei. This functional autonomy provides a clue to why Acer—alone of the Asian PC vendors—has been able to grow significant U.S. market share in desktops and servers.

"We stay in tune with the local marketplace and have the flexibility to do what's necessary to address local requirements," according to Ronald Chwang, president and chief operating officer of Acer America. Chwang, whose U.S. experience includes graduate school at the University of Southern California and stints at Bell Labs and Intel, views Acer America's success as the result of his ability to pursue market strategies that make sense in the United States. Where most other Asian companies tend to keep a tight rein on their American subsidiaries, Chwang has the authority to move his subsidiary America in completely new directions.

Acer's culture is highly decentralized, with most of the power devolving down to the lowest level possible in the corporation. Acer America's CEO Chwang, for example, does not see his job in terms of top-down management control. To Chwang, the job of the CEO is to provide a vision and to communicate that vision both inside and outside the corporation. He sees himself as a team builder, continually motivating employees to align their personal goals with corporate goals. This is the Silicon Valley style of management, imported into a country that's half-way around the world.

Case Study: The Transformation at Wang

Another company that once adhered to the "Employee = Child" mindset was Wang Laboratories, one of the traditional computer vendors blindsided by the growth of the personal computer. Like the other traditional vendors, Wang remained in a state of denial for many years about the impact that the personal computer was having on the computer industry.

Wang's decline was the inevitable result of a business culture that was completely inappropriate for the fastest moving industry in the world. Today's computer industry is marked by short product cycles, rapidly declining prices, multiple competing channels, and sudden market shifts. Only companies that can move quickly to exploit new opportunities can survive, let alone prosper and grow. Successful companies have organizations and processes that are flexible and can adapt.

The old Wang was the antithesis of this. Founded by an autocrat, Wang was organized like an imperial court. It suffered from a complex hierarchy of bureaucrats, each striving to protect and control administrative turf. Battles raged between internal factions, as each manager tried to seize political power.

Meanwhile, the computer industry was changing at light speed, leaving Wang's products far behind, and the company began a long and debilitating decline. Layoff followed layoff. Reorganization and downsizing received far more management attention than products and customers. Eventually, the company had no choice but to declare bankruptcy. The stock, once the darling of Wall Street, became almost worthless.

This change in fortune took a tremendous toll on the engineers, marketers, salespeople and clerical staff who were the foundation of the corporation. Many of the most talented left for other companies. Those that remained harbored extraordinary anger at Wang's management, whose infighting and lack of vision had driven a great corporation into financial disgrace.

However, Wang had one thing going for it—it had "bottomed out." The remaining Wang employees—collectively and individually—knew that *something* had to change.

Today, Wang is a completely different company; it is a *software* company. In a certain sense, this was always the case. It was Wang's excellent word processing software that had made Wang's stand-alone word processing systems so popular, and

Wang had a tradition of creating innovative software for office workers. Essentially, the pain of bankruptcy allowed Wang to realize its true identity. The company issued new stock and found new investors. Wang transformed itself from a near-dead hardware vendor into an interesting software company that's positioned for growth.

One of the leaders key to this amazing turnaround was Dan Cerutti, whom I've quoted earlier. Dan has been something of a professional iconoclast throughout most of his career. At IBM, where he was in charge of the software for IBM's high-powered workstations, he was a vocal and visible opponent of IBM's dress code, and bucked convention by wearing blue jeans when he met with IBM's customers. Dan left IBM to fill the software VP slot at Wang where he played a crucial role in the cultural change process. Dan then left Wang to start his own software company, Amulet, which is building software for the Internet.

I caught up with Dan when he was still software VP at Wang, deep in the thick of Wang's cultural transformation. Dan told me about how he and his colleagues were changing the company:

> We created a cultural revolution at Wang. I don't think that [former CEO] Miller really understood how serious those changes had to be. The people here now are new age information thinkers, and share the same desire for a new Wang. I'm the extreme, and I'm the first to admit it. I brought with me the objective to literally reengineer the culture.

Dan, along with the rest of the management team, painted a picture of a renewed company that resembled Microsoft more than it did the hardware company it once had been. This vision inspired the remaining employees and was momentous enough to bring new talent to the company. Investors got on the bandwagon. At one point, two venture capitalist firms were bidding to give $55 million to get the new company launched. Employees received special founder's stock, thus making the prospect of staying with or joining Wang potentially lucrative.

Wang's management found ways to shake the organization out of its complacency. New staff brought experience to help propel the new direction. Dan Cerutti commented:

> We had to bring in new blood. Not too much, though. A third is about the most any team can absorb, in my experience. Fifty percent is too disruptive. Think about that—for every three people, two have historical continuity. That turns out to be just right.

Wang's management also dismantled the elaborate web of executive privileges and perks that made regular employees feel like underprivileged children. For example, the executive elevator, an express to the headquarters' top-floor executive suite, was converted into a regular elevator. Wang's management also planned events to symbolize the new Wang. Dan Cerutti gave me this example:

> We had a day out in the parking lot, like a celebration. We had a dunk tank, and the people who were dunked were the senior people. The employees loved it. They gathered around to throw balls at the bosses and put them in the water. It was a great thing to do that wouldn't have been possible in the old days.

The way that people treated one another changed, too. Dan Cerutti again:

> Just as significant as the dramatic moves are the little ways you treat people every day. When you stop by people's offices, you just treat them with respect for what they bring to the business. In response, they respect your right to make a decision, your obligation to make a decision.

Wang's journey from being the biggest disaster in the computer industry to (in the words of one analyst) becoming "a billion-dollar start-up" proves that massive corporate cultural change not only is possible, but practical. If Wang, bankrupt and in decline, can rework itself, then any organization can do it.

The key to making such a transformation is to scrap the notion that employees are children and treat them as peers. This new mindset has powerful consequences, as shown in Table 4.1.

Implementation Strategies

Effective managers focus on maintaining this peer structure by hiring people who will be good additions to the existing

· ·

TABLE 4.1
COMPARISON OF CHILD AND PEER MINDSETS

· ·

EMPLOYEE = CHILD

• *Identity.* The ideal employee is a docile conformist, who will obey the rules.

• *Organization.* Structures are set up to control and supervise employee behavior to ensure that all the rules are followed.

• *Motivation.* Employees are assumed to want a reasonable salary, job security, and a company to take care of them.

EMPLOYEE = PEER

• *Identity.* The ideal employee is self-motivated and flexible, and does whatever it takes to make the team successful.

• *Organization.* People form small teams that have complete responsibility for their success within the context of the company's mission.

• *Motivation.* Employees want to change the world and make a difference, with the possibility of making big money somewhere down the line.

· ·

staff. It also means treating employees as if they are as valuable and as important as the managers and shareholders who are running the company, as Stan Shih, CEO of Acer Group, makes clear:

> *The customer comes first, then the employees and then the shareholders. Some companies put the shareholder first. That makes the investors happy but those companies can't survive for ten, twenty, thirty years. They're too concerned with short-term profits to give much attention to growing a business.*

Effective managers inside Silicon Valley business cultures know that it takes constant effort to keep the Employee = Peer mindset active and alive within the corporate culture. Here are three of their strategies:

- *Hire the self-motivated.*
- *Eliminate fancy perks.*
- *Sacrifice the sacred cows.*

Let's look at each of these strategies in more detail.

STRATEGY 10: HIRE THE SELF-MOTIVATED

Being a peer means taking responsibility for your own actions. It takes a special kind of employee to feel comfortable and secure with this attitude. In particular, it requires the ability to stay self-motivated without a supervisor or manager looking over your shoulder. Former Microsoft executive vice president Mike Maples commented on Microsoft's employees:

> *We find people who are very self-motivated, who set their own targets, and then drive themselves to achieve their goals. They're intellectually honest, if you will, in terms of training themselves*

to do better. We look for people who are leaders, who not only are self-motivated but who can help motivate other people.

Traditional companies also look for people who are self-starters, but generally only for positions such as sales that are conducted outside the corporate environment. The challenge is to find self-motivated people at *all* levels of the organization, even for positions that traditional companies would consider low-level labor. Frank Ingari, CEO of Shiva, explained:

> *Self-actualizing behavior is present in a significant minority of the population. It's people on the manufacturing line, the truck drivers, and everybody else. You have to treat them with respect. Everybody's job has merit, and it's amazing what people will do just to be a part of a quality operation that delivers something tangible. People love that. They'll work beyond all expectation.*

Frank makes an important point here that is echoed by many of his colleagues. *Everybody* is important, and an excellent company has to have excellence *everywhere.* That's possible only if everyone (including the people on the loading dock and the people who clean the floors) is doing a top-rate job, without being overseen by paternalistic bureaucrats.

Self-motivation also implies a high level of personal flexibility. This is vital because the duties of any job on a team are likely to change on a week-to-week basis. Many positions don't even have written job descriptions. The idea is that everybody on the team does whatever it takes to get the job done, to get the product out, to make the customer happy. This requires people who are flexible enough to handle ambiguity and, sometimes, chaos. Shiv Nadar, chairman of HCL (India's second largest software design firm), put it this way:

> *We look for employees who are natural entrepreneurs. Markets are always evolving, and entrepreneurs identify these opportunities*

and turn them into businesses. We try to find people who are particularly good at this. On the other hand, we avoid people who rely excessively on past experience. The worst are the one who think that certain things are impossible. Once you say that something is impossible, it can't be done—even if it actually is possible, though it might seem difficult at the time.

Entrepreneur Jonathan Seybold, founder and past president of Seybold Seminars and noted industry guru, commented on the type of person who's a good fit for a Silicon Valley-style organization:

There are people for whom order and continuity and predictability are very important. They're like pets who resent absolutely any variation from their daily routine. At the other end of the spectrum are people who are basically anarchists. Along that continuum are people who like making sense of things but who are comfortable with ambiguity. Life itself can be ambiguous! I try to hire people who can deal with that.

Just as there are types of prospective employees that the Silicon Valley companies seek out, there are those they tend to avoid. For example, they generally don't hire the "professional managers" that are so common in the upper echelon of many of today's companies. An MBA doesn't count for much in the world of high tech. What does count is a solid understanding of products, technology, and the customer needs. This requires a certain level of technical understanding that the so-called professional manager is likely to lack. Former Microsoft VP Mike Maples explained:

We look for people who are highly skilled in their area, but more important, who are extraordinarily smart and can learn. If somebody says he or she is a programmer, we test him or her.

But, often, we'll hire somebody who's not that good a program-
mer, say, but who's smart and willing to commit to learning.
But, we don't hire very many people to come in as managers.
People are hired as marketing people, or as programming peo-
ple, or as content specialists, but not typically as professional
managers.

The trend against hiring professional managers is based on
a concern that such people function professionally in ways
that make sense in traditional environments but that are not
acceptable in a Silicon Valley-style organization. Such techniques tend to create dissent and anger, thereby disconnecting
employees from the higher goals of the corporation. The traditional manager is likely to insist on the same kind of exaggerated respect and obedience that a subordinate historically has
shown a "superior," rather than the mutual respect that exists
between peers.

Organizations with a Silicon Valley business culture are always looking for employees who are entrepreneurs. They want
people who love what they do and are motivated by doing it.
Frank Ingari, CEO of Shiva, defined what he considers the
most valuable kind of employee:

I had a guy in here yesterday. He's 29 years old. He's one of the
head architects in the company. He's had no management train-
ing, none at all. I'm trying to find out what drives the guy, be-
cause he's a very important person for us to maintain and
motivate. He doesn't really care about the money, he just loves
building products. Now that's obviously the gem you're looking
for because he's a born entrepreneur.

The goal, then, is to hire people who are "born entrepreneurs," who can adapt to a new corporate culture without have
to unlearn a lot of bad habits. This can often mean favoring

youth and enthusiasm over age and experience. Hewlett-Packard CEO Lew Platt explained:

Historically, we've tried to recruit top students from top schools. While we do some experienced recruiting, the bulk of it is from college graduates. We find that people who have not spent a lot of time out in the work world come on board and buy into the culture. A lot of things around here just happen because that is the right way to do things at HP. Bringing in young people who don't have old cultural habits to shed before taking on our culture seems to work best for us. Beyond that, we look probably for the same things that other companies look for. That means people who are smart and have the focus to accomplish things. We look for people who are good communicators, who can work well in teams, because more and more, work in companies today is done by teams, not by individuals.

Companies in Silicon Valley generally have long and complex preemployment interviews. It's not unusual for a prospective candidate to interview not just with his or her manager but with prospective peers as well. If the candidate is being considered for a management job, typically, the candidate is interviewed by the people who will report to him or her. These extensive interviews make certain that the candidate will fit into the culture and into the team. As Jonathan Seybold put it:

When you hire people, you have to pay attention to how they're going to fit in. Someone can be a great person, but if he or she is not going to fit into the culture or the team, he or she is the wrong person. In this organization, there is a low tolerance for people who are political, who do not contribute to the team effort, or whose influence is negative. The focus in on getting the job done, and we simply don't have the time for people who violate that.

Strategy 11: Eliminate Fancy Perks

When employees and managers are expected to team up and treat one another as peers, it's obviously hypocritical if the corporation treats some team members (the managers) better than it treats the other team members. This is precisely the reason many high tech organizations limit fancy management perks. Gone are executive washrooms and dining rooms, big offices, and limos that signaled to management and rank and file that managers are superior to workers and thus deserve special treatment. Perks also further isolate executives from the employees, exacerbating the hierarchy. Mitchell Kertzman, CEO of Sybase, commented on the need for a consistent message here:

> It's not fair to expect employees to stay at a Motel 6 while the senior executives are flying around in corporate jets and golfing at the country club. I don't believe that everybody should wear sackcloth, but you've got to be consistent in your message and what you ask people to do. You don't want your average employee thinking that his or her wasting money on a daily basis is irrelevant in the scheme of things compared with executive compensation, executive travel, and executive perks.

Some CEOs don't even have private offices. For example, when Bob Frankenberg joined Novell as CEO, he took up residence in a cubicle—just like everybody else at Novell. Obviously, it isn't that high-tech companies can't afford these extras, it's that a synonym for perks in this context is separateness. I asked Bob Frankenberg if he missed the luxuries that he might have enjoyed at a more traditional firm:

> Fancy perks actually make me feel very uncomfortable. I think that each of us has a job to do, and there isn't any job that isn't important. Or, if there is, then we shouldn't be doing that job. I consider just that we have different roles; there is not a hierarchy. We have

an information system that allows me to implement this new structure. It's a great enabler for productivity.

STRATEGY 12: SACRIFICE THE SACRED COWS

Old habits die hard. Even if an organization is fired up with the possibility of a new culture and is willing to confront the reality of its past failures, some people will continue to behave in ways that are familiar to them. Most organizations—even ones trying to change—are filled with "sacred cows"—old ideas about how management is supposed to be treated. Even when the managers themselves would like this to change, it's often difficult to get employees to truly believe that the managers aren't just pretending.

For example, one of Wang Laboratories' sacred cows was the expected deference shown to management, a holdover from its original, highly autocratic corporate culture. As described earlier, in a symbolic debunking of this practice, employees unceremoniously dunked managers in a tank of water at a company picnic.

There has to be an "in your face" quality to sacrificing a sacred cow. Otherwise, it doesn't serve to interrupt the patterns of behavior in a sufficiently dramatic way. It has to be an act that simultaneously buries the old culture and establishes the new one. To illustrate this, the following true story shows how a single individual can have a major effect on an entire culture.

These events took place at a software development center that was located far from the corporate headquarters of a mainframe manufacturer. About 100 programmers had been working night and day on a very complicated piece of software. Suddenly, top management decided to assign a new director to the center, someone who had been trained at corporate headquarters.

The announcement couldn't have been made at a worse time. There had always been a certain amount of tension between the development center, which was full of counterculture types, and corporate headquarters, which was strictly old school. As a result of this announcement, rumors began to surface that "the development center will be shut down," "the project's going to get canceled," "they'll make everyone wear a tie" and so forth.

One senior programmer quit, and made certain that everyone knew he was taking this action because he disapproved of the change in management. This created even more rumors, more uncertainty. The ambitious deadline was forgotten and work on the software project ground to a halt. A delegation from corporate headquarters were scheduled to visit the development center, to officially hand the reins of power over to the new director. It was, in the minds of the programming staff, the beginning of the end.

One programmer, however, wasn't unsettled by all this organizational brouhaha. He was the project leader, the person responsible for ensuring that the software project was completed on time. From his perspective, the identity of the new director had little to do with getting the software out on time and satisfying the customers who were waiting for delivery. He tried to convince his co-workers that they should continue to work, but to no avail.

Out of frustration, the project leader rented a gorilla costume—a hairy black bodysuit with black rubber hands and feet—and brought it to work on the day that the corporate delegation was scheduled to arrive. He waited until the executives were comfortably settled in the conference room. Then he put on the gorilla suit, and emerged from the bathroom in all his hairy glory. He sped through the hallways, ignoring the gasps of his co-workers and the shriek of a secretary who wandered into his path, and went straight to the conference room, opened the door, and entered.

Twelve executives stared up at him, mouths agape. Growling and huffing, he stumped and shambled around the conference room table doing a fine imitation of a disgruntled gorilla. Then he left without a word, returned to his office, and changed back into his normal T-shirt and blue jeans.

Three things happened as a result of this incident. First, the programmers forgot all about the corporate shake-up and, laughing, returned to work. Second, the new director realized that he wasn't going to be able to manage this group the same way he had managed his group at headquarters. Third, the delegation from corporate headquarters decided that it would be best if they left the development center alone in the future.

The project leader's act became the stuff of legend. With this one dramatic action, the project leader had ensured that the software was released on time, a goal that was, after all, far more critical than a change on an organizational chart.

Of equal importance, the gorilla incident changed the culture of that development center by sacrificing a sacred cow that exists inside many organizations—the notion that politics, not products, are important to success. I'm not suggesting everybody go out and rent gorilla suits. But I am pointing out that individuals have the ability to change an organization's culture. It requires courage and the willingness to take bold, dramatic action.

Sacrificing sacred cows is also more of an art than a science. First you must identify the sacred cows. Then you design a dramatic way to sacrifice each one publicly, so that people can internalize the emotional message of the sacrifice. The specific form of the sacrifice will vary according to the circumstance of the organization and the nature of the sacred cows, but with a little creativity, this strategy can be an effective vehicle for breaking down the barriers between managers and employees.

Employees Are Peers, Not Children

How Evolved Is Your Organization?

The following quiz will help you to assess to what extent your organizational culture considers non-management employees to be important to the success of the organization:

• •

The Following Is True . . .

	Always	Frequently	Sometimes	Seldom	Never
1. Our executives eat apart from the peons.	___	___	___	___	___
2. Taking the initiative is a good way to get promoted.	___	___	___	___	___
3. Our dress code is rigorously followed.	___	___	___	___	___
4. When we have a company party, *everyone* parties.	___	___	___	___	___
5. Somebody is always looking over my shoulder.	___	___	___	___	___
6. I can call anybody here by his or her first name.	___	___	___	___	___
7. Managers make a lot more money than regular folks.	___	___	___	___	___
8. It's normal to say "hello" to the janitorial staff.	___	___	___	___	___
9. The big boss makes all the hiring decisions.	___	___	___	___	___
10. Just about everybody interviews a new team candidate.	___	___	___	___	___

• •

Scoring:

For all odd-numbered statements, score:

Always	1
Frequently	2
Sometimes	3
Seldom	4
Never	5

For all even-numbered statements, score:

Always	5
Frequently	4
Sometimes	3
Seldom	2
Never	1

If your score is 10–20: Your work environment is deeply stratified, with major barriers between management and workers. It's likely that there is deep resentment and hostility between managers and workers. Some workers will goof off if they get half a chance.

If your score is 21–35: Your organization is average. Managers and executives aren't treated like superstars, but they do have a lot of privileges that the rest of the team members lack. Great effort is probably expended securing special perks, like big offices and fancy furniture.

If your score is 36–50: Your organization is close to the Silicon Valley ideal. Workers and managers tend to respect on another and feel that they are contributing—as best they are able—to the shared goals of the organization. Self-motivation and creativity at all levels of the organization is generally rewarded, sometimes quite lavishly.

Points to Ponder

In order to create leverage for change, write out the answers to the following questions:

• What do you feel toward individuals and organizations who make you feel like you are inferior simply because your job is less glamorous than theirs?

_____

_____

_____

_____

_____

• How would your organization perform differently if people really believed that they were peers who shared in the success of the entire team?

_____

_____

_____

_____

_____

• What do you think is the primary psychological motivation behind concepts like "corporate respect" that tend to lionize managers simply for being in management?

_____

_____

_____

_____

_____

- How do you feel when you see somebody enjoying a fancy management perk? Do you want to work harder to make the organization successful, or do you just want to get in on the goodies?

_____

_____

_____

_____

However, even if an organization is treating employees and managers as equally important, people need a reason to "go the extra mile"—to take on challenges that might daunt another organization. In order to make this happen, an organization needs to internalize the fifth key to Silicon Valley culture . . .

Key No. 5

....

MOTIVATE WITH VISION, NOT FEAR

....

The Silicon Valley Mindset: Motivation = Vision

Unquestionably, the most successful leader in the computer industry is Bill Gates, cofounder and chairman of Microsoft, the world's largest independent software company. Bill is both a visionary and a master at getting other people to share his vision of the future. Today, Bill has all the resources of a giant corporation at his back and can spend millions of dollars promoting his vision. But all that power is simply an extension of what Bill has been doing since he was a young boy. Bill's early years as a programmer helped him mold his vision:

> My interest in computers began early, and I started programming in high school at age 13. When I was at Harvard in 1974, Paul Allen and I began the development of BASIC for the first microcomputer, the MITS Altair. Even then we were convinced that the personal computer would ultimately become a valuable tool found on every office desktop and in every home. We saw that a microcomputer revolution was underway, and we left Harvard the following year to form Microsoft in pursuit of that vision.

As Microsoft grew, Bill's vision grew along with it. He has likened the process of building a great company to that of building a program. First comes the vision, which provides the motivation, and then comes the discipline to make the vision into a reality.

> *The ability to recognize opportunities is essential to success in this fast-moving industry. A healthy dose of vision has been central to development of Microsoft. Every decision we make is based on where we think the technology will be five and ten years in the future. Our programming experiences prepared us well for a managerial role. The programmer's ability to envision a strong product and methodically map out the code that must be written to build it is analogous to the manager's ability to envision a strategic new line of business and delineate the appropriate steps to create it.*

According to Bill, one of the reasons that the traditional computer vendors were unable to adapt was that they lost their sense of vision and therefore failed to change as the market did:

> *In this leadership role, I am constantly reminded of the need for clear vision and strong execution. Many companies that were once great powers in this business have lost their way. Fixated on the technology that made them great, they were not able to extend their reach into new areas. At Microsoft I make sure we don't fall short for not having an expansive view of how technology can be used.*

Another high-tech leader who believes in the power of vision is Eckhard Pfeiffer, the CEO of Compaq. When Eckhard took over the leadership of Compaq, the company was in decline. Once famous for developing the best personal computers in the industry, it had lost its edge and was losing market share. Eckhard, however, had a vision of what Compaq could be. He not only believed that Compaq could pull itself out of the doldrums, he knew that Compaq had potential for new growth. He wasn't satisfied with keeping Compaq in the number three market share position in PC sales after industry giants IBM and Apple. Instead, he believed that Compaq could be number one in market share. Within two years, he had turned that vision into a reality. Eckhard commented:

> *From a CEO's perspective, you're taking on a very large respon-*
> *sibility. Ultimately, it's people that make everything happen.*
> *That's what we keep saying, but at times we forget it. You have a*
> *responsibility to shape the vision of a company, and you know*
> *that whatever process you choose will determine ultimately the*
> *well-being of the organization. You have to drive that vision and*
> *long-term strategies and objectives. You deal with it on a day-to-*
> *day basis. And you always have to remember that your competi-*
> *tors are doing the same thing. They're working as intensely on all*
> *these things as well. The element of success is a satisfaction and*
> *gratification for putting in the effort.*

A sense of vision, shared among the employees in an organization, is the best way to motivate people. Of course, they aren't the only business leaders who understand the power of vision. The ability to share a vision is a quality that all great leaders share, including traditional ones. Effective high-tech managers, however, avoid the use of fear to motivate employees.

This isn't to say that companies with a Silicon Valley culture don't fear the competition. In fact, one attribute of a healthy high-tech company according to Intel CEO Andy Grove, is a "healthy sense of paranoia." What's meant by this "paranoia" is a refusal to become complacent and ignore the ever-present threat of new technology and the creativity of other companies in your industry. This kind of "healthy paranoia," however, is worlds away from the fear that's inspired by a manager who tries to terrify his or her employees into submission.

The Traditional Mindset: Motivate = Fear

Probably the most dysfunctional concept of traditional corporate culture is that it's appropriate, even beneficial, to control workers with fear. This concept arises naturally out of the other mindsets that we've discussed already. If the function of management is to control worker behavior, and the way to view employees is as children, then management needs a tool with which to keep the children in line. And, historically, that tool has been fear.

Many managers hold the threat of firing or demotion over employees' heads. The message is clear: "Work hard or you're outta here!" The tone was set in the nineteenth century. Anyone who refused (or was unable) to work fourteen-hours days, seven days a week, was unceremoniously dismissed, only to be replaced by another—to the manager—faceless, nameless laborer.

The all-too-obvious strong-arm tactics were abandoned by the mid-twentieth century. IBM, for example, became known for its policy of lifetime employment. Once you were hired by IBM, you had a steady job for the rest of your life, as long as you followed the rules. IBM, like other companies that promised such security, has been unable to deliver on that promise. Recent changes in the economy have made the concept of a steady job nothing more than a memory. Millions of workers have lost their jobs as a result of downsizing, rightsizing, outsourcing, and reengineering. This resurgence of insecurity in the workplace has reawakened the fear of joblessness in many workers in all fields.

Fear makes companies less competitive and adaptable, and causes workers to become less, rather than more, productive. When people are afraid, they will avoid taking necessary risks. I've worked with companies whose employees are so afraid that it's a miracle anything gets done at all. People in these organizations become paralyzed and won't take any action whatsoever lest they be blamed if it goes awry. Managers start demanding detailed plans for everything in a vain attempt to guarantee that nothing goes wrong. What usually happens in these cases is that the organization ends up studying the possible outcomes of an opportunity so long that the opportunity ceases to exist. Computer industry guru Jonathan Seybold commented:

> *In traditional organizations, people were often punished for taking risks that didn't pan out. Consequently, the major activity in the organization was deflecting blame. So you send memos, you hold meetings, all to make certain that you are "clean." I've seen this to be the case even when the organization was full of bright, literate, intelligent human beings. The culture starts to run them, not the other way around.*

The climate of fear in many companies slows decision making to a crawl while everyone seeks to cover his or her behind. Distrust leads to bureaucracies that insist on checking every last detail. Tasks that, in a reasonable organization, could be handled in a few hours, in such an organization might take days, weeks, or months, or never be completed.

In many traditionally-managed engineering groups, for example, a product can't even be considered for prototyping until there was an engineering plan, a marketing plan, a sales plan, a competitive analysis, a release plan, a master plan, and a project plan, all of which had to be reviewed and approved by multiple departments and bureaucracies. Since it literally took months to create and review all these documents, it was rarely possible to get products launched in a timely fashion, which is critical in that market. In addition, the homework had to be repeated at each stage of the development process, so that a product was never complete until it had hundreds of signatures and sign-offs. Projects that should have taken months stretched into years, or got caught in an endless maze of paperwork and politics. And, by the time the rare product actually did get built, it was out of date.

Fear also degrades the quality of communications inside an organization. In an effort to deflect potential blame, employees engage in double-talk and "weasel words." Whenever you see a memorandum that's a soup of industry buzzwords and half-truths, carefully crafted to spread blame and communicate next to nothing, you can bet that there's a terrified executive or two cowering nearby. Here's an example:

After due consideration of alternatives, we take calculated risks based on a wise assessment of market conditions.

No doubt, the executives who wrote this felt that they were making a strong statement. But between the lines, the message is: "We don't take risks."

One of the most ridiculous manifestations of motivation by fear is a function called "group writing." A group of professionals sit together in a meeting and try to write a paragraph. In the quest for perfect phrasing, they debate and comment on each word. It can take an hour to do a single sentence, a day to do a paragraph. The reason for this bizarre ritual is to make certain that everyone is "happy" with the wording, meaning that everyone agrees to share the blame for what it says. And if *everyone* shares the blame, then *no one* is responsible if things go wrong.

The result of double-talk and group writing is that people in an organization stop valuing truth, even if they can still recognize it. Information that is difficult for the culture to absorb gets buried and avoided. Over time, managers and employees alike lose track of what's going on in the market because everybody's afraid to state the facts.

Employees who are afraid don't make good decisions, they don't take well-considered risks, and they don't act rationally. Go into almost any conference room in a traditionally run company and you'll see them. They glance around the room frequently, waiting and worrying, laughing a little too loudly when the boss cracks a feeble joke, agreeing with whatever idea seems popular or politically correct.

In contrast, companies that manage according to Silicon Valley principles believe that they will succeed or fail based on the ability—and willingness—of their employees to take intelligent risks. They know there simply isn't time in this fast-changing economy to study a problem to death, to engage in complicated consensus building, or to be afraid. Bold behavior is impossible when people in an organization are fearful of the consequences if they make a mistake. Consequently, effective high-tech managers don't expect perfection from their employees. They only expect people to learn from their mistakes. Powersoft CEO Mitchell Kertzman comments:

> I can't imagine motivating people through fear. You don't want people afraid of the consequences if they screw up. I want them to do the right thing, but if they try to do the right thing and fail, I still want them to try. Everybody is allowed mistakes. That's not to say that people are allowed to make the same mistake over and over again. The first mistake is almost always forgiven, especially if the person can learn from the experience.
>
> You don't want people to work in a risk-averse culture. You don't want someone, for example, to come up with an idea and have everybody else in the room say (or imply): "That's the dumbest thing I've ever heard and, boy, are you a stupid person." If you do that, the person will never again come up with an idea for fear that it might be laughed at. We have a very demanding culture, and ideas get put on the table, including my own, to which people say, essentially, "that's a dumb idea," but they're not saying "you're a stupid person."

Rather than increasing the level of fear in the organization, effective managers seek to minimize it. They want employees to feel that they are in charge of their destiny—not waiting for the proverbial axe to drop. They want employees to claim ownership for their decisions, not seek to pass or share blame. This means that they must depend on a shared vision, rather than on fear, to provide the primary motivation. The different effects of Motivation = Fear and Motivation = Vision are shown in Table 5.1.

The impact of Motivation = Fear shows itself most clearly in the quality of life in the corporation. Fear always makes employees miserable and unhappy.

Work in a high-tech organization can be a wonderful and positive experience. My first job was at the Los Angeles Development Center, an organization that was ahead of its time in terms of its organizational culture. Dress was casual, everyone

------

TABLE 5.1
COMPARISON OF FEAR AND VISION MINDSETS

MOTIVATION = FEAR

- *Mistrust and Distrust.* Fear makes it difficult to trust your colleagues, peers, and employees, who are assumed either to be enemies or (at best) temporary allies.
- *Predictability.* Frightened people don't like surprises, so they set up structures to make sure that everything remains completely under control, that is, unchanging.
- *Deceptiveness.* In fearful organizations, employees consider it appropriate and even wise to deflect blame by fabricating or omitting information.

MOTIVATION = VISION

- *Trust.* A shared vision makes it easier to trust the colleagues who share your hopes and dreams in the context of the organization's larger goals.
- *Courage.* A shared vision encourages people to take necessary risks and to do what it takes to make the vision into a reality.
- *Decisiveness.* A shared vision creates a work environment in which decisions can be made quickly and easily because it's clear how each decision fits into the overall vision.

------

was on a first-name basis, and crack programmers held more power than managers. Most important, the group had a mission that permeated every aspect of daily working life. This mission consisted of a commitment to achieve a goal that no software development organization had ever done before—rewrite the programming code for a complex, multiuser operating system so that it would run on a completely different hardware platform. It was a project that many computer scientists considered impractical, if not impossible, especially in the timeframe (three years) allotted.

Rather than being daunted by the size of the task, we were empowered by a sense of adventure, for we were exploring new ground, accomplishing something unique. Motivated by that vision, we worked long hours, often 50 to 60 a week, and yet few of us were conscious of how hard we were working. And on Monday mornings, we looked forward to going back to work. My job was far from the most important in the organization (I was a new hire just out of college), but I was made to feel as if I were an essential part of the teams on which I served. I was free to attend any meeting that interested me or at which I felt I could make a contribution. The camaraderie spilled over into our personal lives; there was a party nearly every weekend, where we'd socialize and talk about the next stage of the development process.

The entire focus of the organization was getting a product out the door. There were about 100 programmers, and only four secretaries. The managers were all former programmers who were capable of making technical contributions. Even the technical writers were expected to know how to program.

The ultimate payback came when we accomplished what had seemed to outsiders to be impossible. Not only did we convert the operating system to the new hardware platform, but we did it on schedule, hitting a deadline that had been set three years earlier. It was an extraordinary triumph and garnered major financial benefits for the parent company.

Whenever I talk to people in companies that have a Silicon Valley culture—regardless of the industry they're in—I sense this same level of energy, dedication, and enthusiasm that is generated when people know that they're part of something special, that they're changing the world, if only in a small way. I can see how a Bill Gates (Microsoft), a Bob Frankenberg (Novell), or an Edward McCracken (Silicon Graphics) can inspire employees to ever-greater achievements.

The key to implementing a vision is, of course, teamwork. The words *team* and *teamwork* can be interpreted differently. A more traditional manager might seek out employees who are team players, but if the manager believes Motivation = Fear, a good team player to that manager will be somebody who doesn't make waves, follows orders from management, and doesn't try to change the status quo. The team is assumed to be the corporation itself, replete with all the control mechanisms and bureaucracies that make it so awkward and unwieldy.

By contrast, to the effective manager who believes Motivation = Vision, a good team player will be somebody who takes the initiative and does whatever it takes to help a small group of like-minded individuals achieve success and renown. The team player in a Silicon Valley-style organization might even be considered a disruptive factor in a more traditional business environment.

Vision and fear are mutually exclusive. An organization that is afraid isn't going to be able to make the changes required to implement *any* vision. A friend of mine was recently employed at a local aerospace plant. It was a typical traditional "big business" organization; managers were clearly bosses, employees were treated as children. Morale and productivity at the plant were low, so the company hired a management consultant to help turn things around. This consultant convinced the plant manager that he needed to communicate a sense of his "vision" to the rest of the workers. The plant manager thus decided to have a "free hot dog day" at the cafeteria. When the workers were eating their free hot dogs, the plant manager emerged from the executive dining room and visited each table, delivering a prepared speech about his "vision" for the corporation. However, because the employees were so used to seeing the plant manager as an ogre who fired people, they barely heard what he was saying. The result was a further drop in morale.

It doesn't have to be that way. Effective managers inspire their organizations with a clear vision of what the company is and where it is going. Employees at successful companies have a clear understanding of what they are trying to accomplish and use that understanding as a touchstone for their everyday behavior. One way that companies with a Silicon Valley culture create a sense of mission is by organizing employees into teams that function like small businesses. This allows each employee to see clearly that his or her action really makes a personal and professional difference.

Effective companies also foster in their employees the belief that if they can't change the world, they can at least make a difference. Former Microsoft executive vice president Mike Maples put it this way:

> *Great companies have people who are smart, energetic, focused, dedicated to the company, and care about what they're doing; they believe that they really are on a mission to change things, and that they're doing what's right for the world and right for humankind.*

Many organizations solidify their missions by developing mission statements. The following are examples of the terminology and thoughts used to inspire employees:

- *Dell Computer.* Develop quality products and do whatever it takes to please the customer.
- *Shiva.* Provide secure, easy-to-use, scalable, and cost-effective remote access solutions that meet the needs of nontechnical end users and network managers alike.

- *Hewlett-Packard.* Provide products and services of the highest quality and the greatest possible value to our customers, thereby gaining and holding their respect and loyalty.
- *Knowledge Adventure.* Make really inspiring, compelling, exciting, multimedia, educational software for kids.

All of these informal mission statements highlight giving something important to the customer, providing a high level of quality, or performing an important service. Placing the mission statement in the context of changing the world—however small this change might be—engenders loyalty to the goals and purpose of the organization.

For companies that manage according to Silicon Valley principles, a mission statement is a crystallization of what the organization is trying to accomplish and why. The goal is to get people thinking about possibilities, rather than limitations. A strong mission statement inspires as much as it informs. Employees must feel that the organization has a goal beyond that of making a profit. A successful statement explains why the organization's products or services make sense not only from a financial viewpoint but also from the viewpoint of the organization's customers.

Case Study: The Renaissance at Compaq

In 1982, a tiny computer start-up called Compaq was founded in Texas by a group of engineers from Texas Instruments who had originally sketched out a plan on a cafeteria napkin. Compaq's follow-on products were so successful that the company made $111 million in the first year. Compaq quickly became the major alternative to IBM as a supplier of personal computers.

Compaq also developed a reputation for building the most advanced and most reliable computers in the marketplace. It forged alliances with retail outlets, making it easy for business-people to purchase Compaq products. It provided telephone support both to the dealers and the customers, so that they could get their computers up and running quickly. Compaq beat IBM to the punch with the first computer based on Intel's 386 chip and issued a portable computer long before IBM. By 1988, Compaq had become the first company in the world to exceed $2 billion in sales within six years.

By 1990, however, the momentum had shifted. Customer requirements and expectations had changed, and Compaq had failed to acknowledge this. Lower-priced, industry-standard PCs had become widely available, but Compaq persisted in delivering premium-priced products. Eventually, the company found itself with uncompetitive products, high product costs, a high-margin pricing structure, and high overhead. Further, in a series of moves that baffled industry analysts, Compaq invested in technology that had nothing to do with its core market.

Compaq's problems reflected its corporate culture, which had been slowly degenerating to resemble the traditional companies to whom it was selling the bulk of its computers. A former employee quoted in *BusinessWeek* (November 2, 1992) summarized the Compaq of 1990: "A slickness came into Compaq. All of a sudden, if you didn't have a MBA, red suspenders, and these little Gucci slippers, you were nobody." In the words of one industry analyst: "Compaq had gone over to the dark side of the force."

Fortunately for Compaq and its shareholders, a new leader emerged to revitalize the company. Eckhard Pfeiffer, who had built and run Compaq's European organization in the 1980s, and who had internalized a positive view of change. Here's what he told me about the nature of change in the computer industry:

Change needs to be constantly on the agenda. We ask everybody: how do we need to do things, not only tomorrow but beyond tomorrow? We've mastered the incredible growth we've had in the last two and a half years with the systems and processes we have, but then outgrew them. We adapt as we move along.

A realist, Eckhard knows that change is the essence of the Information Age:

This is an industry that has gone through dramatic change and, with all probability, will continue to do so. Ten years ago, IBM was leading, and Digital was doing its thing, but the seeds of change had already been planted with the appearance of the personal computer. The speed of change is not just evolutionary; it is revolutionary. It cannot be predicted. Many may take a stab at it and try to predict which way it's going to work out, but the forces are powerful, and the different kinds of industries coming together are creating something entirely new.

In response to what he was witnessing, Eckhard changed the direction of Compaq. According to *BusinessWeek* (November 2, 1992), the deciding moment was when Pfeiffer declared that Compaq would match the price of any manufacturer in the world. As a premier engineering company that made the "highest of high-tech" PCs, this was a radical statement, running contrary to almost everything that Compaq had stood for. Eckhard then set an even more extravagant goal. He announced to his employees—and the world—that Compaq could, and would, outsell all other manufacturers of personal computers by 1996.

Eckhard next instructed his executives to cut costs from 35 to 50 percent so that Compaq could compete everywhere that people bought personal computers. He knew that if Compaq was going to grow, it would have to produce personal computers that appealed to everyone, not just to its corporate consumers of the past. This bold strategy required Compaq to alter most of its makeup: manufacturing, marketing, engineering, sales, support.

Previously, Compaq's salesforce had sold primarily to corporate buyers. Now the base was expanded to include retailers and other distributors that catered to nonbusiness consumers. This required different skill sets, different business contacts, and different ways of deploying sales resources.

Similarly, to manufacture personal computers that had a lower price point (a requirement in the home market) Compaq had to find ways to economize on manufacturing without sacrificing overall quality. This required a greater amount of outsourcing of manufacturing to foreign countries, where certain components could be manufactured more cheaply. Again, this required new skills, new business contacts, new ways of deploying manufacturing resources and new ways of managing the flow and supply of parts.

The changes at Compaq were just as radical in the area of customer support. The company had to prepare itself for the kind of customer hand-holding that's necessary when selling computers to the general public. The business buyer often has a staff of computer professionals on which to rely for basic support. Not so for Jane and John Q. Public, who must turn to the manufacturer when they encounter difficulties. The cost of providing that level of support had to be factored into the margins for consumer products, thereby exacting even greater demands to keep costs down.

It is difficult to overestimate the impact of these changes on the daily activities of the Compaq staff. The company achieved Eckhard's ambitious goal two years early. In 1994, Compaq sold more dollars' worth of personal computers than any other company in the world. Eckhard Pfeiffer comments:

We created a new direction and new goals that people could visualize and identify with, and that intuitively sounded right to them. That doesn't mean just going with the majority. It must be right. Then you can communicate it well and get people to "buy in." Then, it's a matter of maintaining the momentum, and making it happen with excitement and good performance—meeting schedules and taking ownership.

Implementation Strategies

The best source of motivation is a sense of vision that brings people together. It describes how being connected with the larger organization has a positive social and career benefit. When people join such an organization, they should feel that they've become part of something that's special, that they have a unique and important purpose that is not only going to enrich their own lives, but make the world a better place. Inside such organizations, it is possible to implement the following business strategies:

- *Create a climate of trust.*
- *Compensate for missions accomplished.*
- *Ruthlessly prioritize.*

STRATEGY 13: CREATE A CLIMATE OF TRUST

I once knew a manager who would periodically complain to his underlings that they weren't telling him the truth. He insisted that he needed good information in order to make good decisions. This wasn't an unreasonable request on the surface. This manager, however, was the same one who every six weeks roped the entire department into helping him prepare a presentation for his management, a presentation that was full of major distortions. As hypocritical as I thought this guy was, I now understand more fully his dilemma. We were all inside a corporation that completely lacked any sense of vision; instead, we were all worrying about whether we'd get fired.

Under the circumstances, distorting the truth became an almost automatic response.

When there's a true sense of vision, on the other hand, and employees know that they're involved in something special, their perspective has balance. When co-workers believe that they're part of a community, they view their colleagues as friends rather than competitors. And managers who don't try to control employee behavior reap the benefits of production inspired out of loyalty, not fear. Stan Shih, CEO of Acer Group, put it this way:

> *Leadership is the process of achieving a dream together, especially when that dream seems impossible to achieve. Leaders have to be open minded, and have to accept the ideas of others, even when they might lead to mistakes. The best training for leadership is to learn from your mistakes. This means that leaders never argue and they never try to shift blame onto others. When something goes wrong a leader always asks "what's wrong with me," not "what's wrong with them."*

These are the components in a climate of trust, without which there can be no vision. Trust is the fertile ground in which the vision is planted, and the fruit that eventually results. Software entrepreneur Dan Cerutti commented:

> *I've known bosses who distrust people and think they won't deliver. It comes through in everything they do. They're afraid to let go. They don't make people feel good. That was true at IBM, and it's still true at many companies. I prefer flat organizations, because you don't need a lot of managers if you trust in the people to do their jobs. It creates faster decision making. You get more autonomy and more responsibility closer to the people who actually know the details. It's these people who need to be empowered to make decisions, then they'll make decisions more quickly, and*

you get a faster heartbeat. You get people who are more responsi-
ble. You get everything I want.

Trust means letting employees make decisions even if those
decisions aren't part of the company's normal practice. It also
means that managers should let go of their fears of anything
out of the ordinary. Sybase's CEO Mitchell Kertzman commented:

> *Suppose I have an employee who's with a customer. It's late in*
> *the evening and the customer has a problem, and the employee—*
> *to do the right thing for the customer—has to give him or her*
> *something or make a commitment that costs money. I want that*
> *employee to do the right thing for the customer, even if it's not*
> *normal practice. He or she wouldn't get punished for that, even*
> *though we might not normally make that kind of commitment. If*
> *it was the right thing to do for that customer at that time, then it*
> *was the right thing to do.*

This is a frightening idea for many managers, especially if they
still define their function as one of control. However, trust
flourishes when managers stop clinging to outmoded roles.
The idea is to inspire and coach rather than to boss and berate.

But even traditional managers can see the logic of "letting
go" when they realize that creating a climate of trust is that it
saves money over the long haul. Here's how Shiv Nadar,
Chairman of HCL (India's second largest software house)
puts it:

> *Bureaucracies indicate a lack of trust and mutual regard and re-*
> *spect. Looking over peoples' shoulders all the time simply does not*
> *work. You introduce a layer of cost that adds no value the moment*
> *a manager thinks his job is to ask employees: "Did you do 'X'?" I*
> *know of one company that was so mistrustful and disrespectful of*

its employees that it spent $5 million overseeing a project that was worth exactly $5 million. Needless to say, that wasn't cost-effective.

STRATEGY 14: BUILD A SHARED VISION

The goal is to create a *shared* vision for your particular organization. To accomplish this, the team must work together to create a sense of vision that reflects the best of all your ideas. A vision can't just be something that comes down from top management; everyone who plays a leadership role must participate to some degree. Former Lotus CEO Jim Manzi put it this way:

> *It's insane to think that cultural change can come directly from a top-down structure, or that there's a monopoly on good ideas at the top of the company.*

When you find influential individuals in the organization who can't or won't cooperate, it's up to you to help bring them into the fold. Some people can be more difficult than others. With a little patience, however, you'll find that almost anyone can be brought around. This may mean a certain amount of gentle persuasion, according to Masayoshi Son, CEO of SOFTBANK:

> *When changing a company, you've got to explain your philosophy and approach. That way people can gradually digest the new culture, which may take some years to implement. The new culture must be based upon what makes sense for the status of your business. For example, within SOFTBANK in Japan, we started forming one division into small teams, and then another, and now it feels natural to the entire organization.*

One of the most wonderful human characteristics is the capacity to adapt and change, to use intellect and emotion to create new environments. Even the most conservative corporate bureaucrat would love to find a deeper sense of joy and excitement in his or her work. Given a choice, most people would prefer to work in an environment where there is a profound understanding of where that organization is going and what will happen when it arrives. Compaq CEO Eckhard Pfeiffer put it this way:

> *Ultimately, it's people that make everything happen. That's what we keep saying, but at times we forget it. You have a responsibility to shape the vision of a company, and realize that whatever process you choose will determine the well-being of the organization. You have to drive that vision along with long-term strategies and objectives, and deal with it on a day-to-day basis. And never forget that your competitors are doing the same thing.*

However, the key to creating a compelling vision of the future is to make certain that the vision translates into real action. Unless people see that the new business strategies are really going to work, then the vision will remain sterile. If you want to create a team that can truly succeed, the team members will have to be ruthless about weeding out old behaviors, rules, structures, standard operating procedures, bureaucracies, and other elements of the old culture that prevent the vision from becoming a reality. Dan Cerutti, former Wang vice president, commented on the need to continually question old ways:

> *Every day, you have to teach people a different way to do business. It means questioning. I question everything. Somebody comes in with some process and says, "We need to do this." I just ask, "Why?" If the answer is something like, "Because that's the*

way we do things here," it's generally something that's only a waste of time. If it can't pass the "why" test, then it's probably work that can be eliminated. In other words, people may have lost track of why they are doing something, although there might have been a very good reason 10, 15 years ago.

This means tirelessly promoting and encouraging behaviors that reinforce the new vision. Here's the advice of former Microsoft vice president Mike Maples:

Corporate culture allows you to move in a direction. It's the belief system that people filter their actions through. In order to change the way a company reacts or behaves, you really have to change the corporate culture. In most cases, companies tend to move from a more freeform to a more structured organization. The entrepreneurs start it, but the venture capitalists or the stockholders replace the management with somebody who's more control-oriented and more process-oriented. So you're continually marching toward more control and more process. If you're going to perform a cultural transplant in a company, that's what you've got to reverse. You've got to decide what the cultural behaviors are that you stand for. If I had a company and was tasked with changing the culture, I would make sure that I understood exactly the current culture. I would communicate thoroughly to the employees what part of the culture we were keeping and what part we were changing and what we were changing it to. Then I'd go overboard in reinforcing the culture that we wanted to move to. Any time there was a borderline decision or a borderline process, I'd overachieve to the new culture.

One of the most serious barriers to establishing a new vision is denial that there is a problem with the status quo. When an organization is "in denial," it precludes an accurate evaluation of the facts. Eckhard Pfeiffer, CEO of Compaq, commented:

You have to stop the denial process, which is hard because it's not something intentional. It is a mindset. Therefore, I test it every day. I'm always asking: Are we in a state of denial in any of our activities? Are we doing things just because we've always done it that way? You have to be willing to come to the conclusion that you might not have the right strategy, might not have the right product, might not have the right cost, might not have the right distribution concept, or the right alliances, or the right technology.

Good examples of debilitating corporate denial are the American automobile manufacturers. How long did it take them to act on consumer demand for reliable cars that didn't guzzle gas? Ten years? Fifteen years? And let us not forget IBM. Big Blue took its first big loss in 1991. At that time, CEO John Akers characterized the problem as a "difficult economy," even though companies such as Microsoft and Intel were posting gigantic growth and profits that same year. IBM had to lose $15 billion over three years before management admitted that something was wrong with IBM, not with the economy. That's a pricey wake-up call, and could have been avoided if IBM's management had confronted reality from the start.

Companies that have a long tradition of success often have the most difficulty acknowledging that what used to work no longer does. Too often, as in the case of IBM, change has to be forced on them. It takes major losses, massive layoffs, and even bankruptcy before most companies begin to come to grips with the need for change. And by then, it may be too late. Compaq CEO Eckhard Pfeiffer comments on anticipating change:

It's easier to get it done [effect change] when you are in a state of crisis. The real challenge comes when you are steaming right along and everybody is preoccupied with getting the job done and you have to ask, are they still keeping their eyes and ears open for the changes that come very rapidly in this industry? Are they looking to the next design cycle or the one beyond that?

STRATEGY 15:
COMPENSATE FOR MISSIONS ACCOMPLISHED

As important as a vision is in achieving success, it won't pay the rent. Employees have to be compensated when the company succeeds. There's a tradition in Silicon Valley companies—especially start-ups—to give employees attractive stock options that, should the company or the project prove successful, can be far more valuable than a high salary. This allows smaller companies to attract top talent, even when they can't afford to pay them a lot of money up front.

Compensation in companies with Silicon Valley business cultures tends to be tied directly to the success of the company (if the company is small) or the success of a product (if the company is large). Effective leaders feel that this is essential to keep people connected to the organization. That connectedness is enhanced when the employee is convinced that his or her contribution directly impacts profitability. It obviously increases productivity when the employee knows that this contribution will result in a higher level of personal compensation.

That's an important component of employee loyalty, according to Stan Shih, CEO of Acer Group:

> *You create employee loyalty through a common vision and strategy. This must be reinforced, however, by the common interest, which means that people must have incentives, stock options and profit-sharing that matches their level of risk. Loyalty also comes from protecting the interests and position of managers and employees when they make mistakes. People really appreciate the opportunity to learn from their mistakes.*

Compensating based on missions accomplished also encourages an atmosphere of thrift, because compensation is tied to the profitability of the team's project. This creates a natural resistance to wasting money. Many high tech companies are among the most profitable in the world. Microsoft, for example, regularly achieves net margins in excess of 25 percent, a figure that's higher than the gross margins for many other industries.

Effective high-tech leaders build cost control into their cultures, so that each individual instinctively keeps an eye on the bottom line. Jonathan Seybold describes the way that he set up his Seybold Seminars company:

> We have a tradition of profit sharing. That was a goal from the start. I believe that the people who are making a business successful should share in that success. One of the consequences is that we've built a culture that is "cheap"—people don't waste money. I didn't realize it when I started, but one of the reasons that so many companies have problems controlling costs is that they try to control them from the top down—with rules and regulations. When you control costs from the bottom up, you don't need all of that. I didn't start profit sharing for that reason, but it was one of the consequences. It breeds a very different kind of organization.

STRATEGY 16: RUTHLESSLY PRIORITIZE

Keeping focused is one of the most difficult things for anybody in today's business world. So much information is thrown at us every day, and there is always more to do than can be done in a single day, week, month, or year. The key to coping with all of this is personal organization, according to software venture capitalist Ann Winblad:

> Personal organization is key to survival. I have voice mail. I have electronic mail. I have Federal Express. I have the mailman. And, by the end of the day, my desk is crowded. If I did not have good personal organization skills, I'd be toast. It is a requirement in flat, free-flowing, participatory organizations. People who have

*great personal organization skills and can manage the overload
are the people who stand out.*

The problem with this advice is that, in order to keep organized, a person needs to know what's high priority and what's not. That's very difficult inside an organization that is confused and that lacks a clear mission. In this case, any information could be valuable or worthless because there's no touchstone for what's important and what's not.

On the other hand, an organization that knows where it's going can easily give its team members the power to differentiate and prioritize. Observe how Scott McNealy, CEO of Sun Microsystems, deals with information pollution:

> *I've never known anybody to fail because they had too much information to make a decision. I think e-mail is great, but because I can speed-read, any topic I'm not interested in, I click, and it's gone. If it's something I need to know, I read it immediately. If it's something I can deal with later, I either print it out or load it into a laptop and take it with me. I've never had too much information.*

The same is true in day-to-day business activities, such as meetings, according to former Microsoft executive vice president Mike Maples commented:

> *You must decide that there are some debates that, while you might be able to contribute and while they are important, you just don't have the time to become involved in. You become an observer or you ignore them.*

The ability to prioritize—and thus be truly productive—is entirely dependent upon the ability to motivate with a clear and understandable vision of what the organization is all about and what needs to happen to make it successful.

How Evolved Is Your Organization?

The following quiz will help you to assess to what extent your organization culture considers non-management employees to be important to the success of the organization:

• •

The Following Is True . . .

	Always	Frequently	Sometimes	Seldom	Never
1. When I go to work, there's a sinking feeling in my gut.	____	____	____	____	____
2. I understand and buy into my group's goals.	____	____	____	____	____
3. Our top management tells us what our "vision" is.	____	____	____	____	____
4. Top management really listens to what we have to say.	____	____	____	____	____
5. People laugh up their sleeves at our "corporate mission."	____	____	____	____	____
6. I can see how working here is growing my career.	____	____	____	____	____
7. Our managers would use layoffs to drive behavior.	____	____	____	____	____
8. Even when things are hectic, I know that we're on track.	____	____	____	____	____
9. There's so much trivial information that I'm swamped.	____	____	____	____	____
10. I make more money if my team accomplishes its mission.	____	____	____	____	____

• •

Scoring:

For all odd-numbered statements, score:

Always	1
Frequently	2
Sometimes	3
Seldom	4
Never	5

For all even-numbered statements, score:

Always	5
Frequently	4
Sometimes	3
Seldom	2
Never	1

If your score is 10–20: Your organization is almost paralyzed with fear. You have little idea where the company is going—other than down the toilet. You feel trapped and wish that you had the opportunity to work elsewhere.

If your score is 21–35: Your organization is average. There's a balance of fear and inspiration, feelings that sometimes cancel each other out. You'd like to believe your group's mission statement but it seems a bit hypocritical. You don't always know what's important and what's not, so its hard to prioritize.

If your score is 36–50: Your organization is close to the Silicon Valley ideal. People aren't afraid to make decisions and then stand by them. It's easy to prioritize because you know exactly what's important to you, to your tem and to the entire corporation.

Points to Ponder

In order to create leverage for change, write out the answers to the following questions:

- If you or somebody on your team saves the company money, is it reflected in your paycheck? Are people rewarded for saving money or penalized for not spending their entire budget at year's end? What would have to change for your organization to make bottom-up cost control a reality?

  _____

  _____

  _____

  _____

  _____

- What action could you take today to reduce or eliminate the level of fear inside your team and inside your entire organization?

  _____

  _____

  _____

  _____

  _____

- Does everyone get the same benefits, or are certain "stars" singled out for extra reward? How does that affect the team?

  _____

  _____

  _____

  _____

  _____

• How much more productive do you think your organization could be if people knew that they'd be rewarded much more lavishly if the organization truly fulfilled its mission?

_____

_____

_____

_____

_____

However, even with a sense of vision that's free from fear, an organization can only reach the highest levels of productivity when people are enjoying their work. In order for this to take place, the people inside the organization must really experience the sixth key to Silicon Valley culture . . .

Key No. 6

....

CHANGE IS GROWTH, NOT PAIN

....

The Silicon Valley Mindset: Change = Growth

High-tech companies are eternal pioneers of the technological frontier, whose boundaries cannot be mapped, because they are constantly expanding. Bill Gates put it succinctly:

> *The human experience is about to change. The transition will be exciting and historic, empowering to individuals, and brutal to some companies and institutions that don't keep pace. Even with the current information highway mania, the impact that emerging digital tools will have and the richness they will bring to people is wildly underestimated. Once certain thresholds are crossed, the way we work and live will change, forever.*

Edward McCracken, CEO of Silicon Graphics, added:

> *The computer industry is in its infancy even though it's been around for forty or fifty years, depending on how you count it. I believe that advanced applications are just starting to be developed and that the next ten or twenty years will be a wonderful time to try new things. And how wonderful and stimulating to be forced continually to change.*

McCracken, Gates, and their peers regard change as exciting, challenging, part of the "juice" of being in business. This attitude is an essential element in their success. They make change a part of their day-to-day business.

This posture enables Silicon Valley-style organizations to continually evolve to meet new circumstances. They transform themselves with relative ease, even when the change presents serious management challenges, such as necessary layoffs. Because such companies have internalized the mental framework that supports a positive view of change, they can make it serve their higher goals. Frank Ingari, CEO of Shiva, explained how this attitude differs from traditional approaches to change:

> *One can deplore the current state of change. That's what the unions do; they have a wrong mental model of reality, of economic reality. Society at large has to embrace change, as opposed to embracing static thinking. Remember the conflict between the steelworkers and the steel mills? How quaint that battle seems today. People are finally realizing that major corporations are not omnipotent; the mighty have fallen. They've had to do horrendous layoffs and the management ended up looking like Bozos. The image of the omnipotent company in a static world making widgets is dead. Today, the reality is constant change and the challenge is who's going to reap the harvest of change.*

Companies with Silicon Valley business cultures are well positioned to harvest the fruits of change became they promote the belief that Change = Growth. That's very different from the dominant attitude of the past.

The Traditional Mindset: Change = Pain

Traditional corporate culture is skeptical and fearful of change. This attitude developed in the nineteenth century, which was a time of social and political turmoil, in the midst of which large corporations seemed like havens of stability. To this day, many corporations use the number of decades they've been in business to promote their value. They enshrine portraits of their founders on the walls of their boardrooms. It even slips into the vocabulary; it's not unusual to hear executives call their company "The Firm" as if to emphasize its rigidity.

To traditionalists, fundamental corporate change should be considered only when the "corporate machine" breaks down, or when the "army" loses the final "battle," or when the company becomes completely "out of control." Change is never regarded as positive; it's always a last resort.

Even the most conservative traditionalists are becoming aware their corporations must change in order to adapt to new markets. This awareness, growing in the late 1980s and early 1990s, led to the popularity of two management techniques—reengineering and total quality management—each promising to help executives transform and update their organizations. However, the traditional corporation's emotional attachment to stability can easily frustrate even well-meaning change attempts.

As defined by Hammer and Champy, in *Reengineering the Corporation* (Harper Business, 1993), reengineering a company "means tossing aside old systems and starting over. It involves going back to the beginning and inventing a better way of doing work." While this sounds good, in practice reengineering has often proven difficult to implement. Even reengineering experts admit that reengineering isn't a panacea:

> We believe that the failure rate for reengineering is, in fact, much higher—on the order of 70 percent. Why do the best-laid reengineering plans often go astray? The causes are many. Despite bold initial pronouncements of shaking up the status quo, some companies end up merely tinkering with well-entrenched business processes. Others try to drive radical process change

from the bottom up and quickly get stymied by functional man-
agers defending parochial interests. And in a few organizations
we have encountered, reengineering is just one more change
program on the corporate agenda, eventually suffocating from
lack of resources and attention. (Steven Stanton, Michael Ham-
mer, and Bradford Power, quoted in Insights Quarterly, *Fall*
Issue, 1992)

The reason that true reengineering is so difficult is that traditional corporate culture places such a high value on stability
that radical change is simply too threatening to be taken on.
The status quo must be defended at all costs, even if the status
quo is slowly destroying profitability.

As a result, many reengineering efforts are doomed to be
ineffective from the start. I once observed from a distance a
reengineering effort conducted by a prestigious management
consulting company. The organization being reengineered
saw the consultants as intruders and there was massive resistance to the process. It quickly degenerated into a seemingly
endless series of meetings, ostensibly to determine how the
organization was currently performing. The output of these
meetings was a gigantic stack of diagrams.

Further meetings took place in which the diagrams were
redrawn to look as different as possible, even though the
processes they described remained the same. A workflow
originally shown as a straight line, for example, was redrawn
as a "closed-feedback" circle, a tree-shaped organization chart
was redrawn as an interconnected pyramid, and so forth. Im-
portant-sounding but ultimately meaningless buzzwords
were liberally sprinkled throughout.

The entire reengineering effort had consumed thousands of
valuable hours of employee time and had cost over a million
dollars in consultant fees. However, the end result—a complicated and nearly unreadable report—was never acted on. The
status quo remained impervious.

Total quality management (TQM) is another corporate change method that hasn't lived up to its promise. TQM was pioneered by the late W. Edwards Deming and Joseph Juran and was widely credited with improving Japanese manufacturing. It uses teams drawn from all parts of the company to define and solve problems, providing statistical analysis tools to track the progress of the change process.

However, despite its initial promise, TQM is beginning to look like a fad whose time has come and gone. As early as October 1995, *USA Today* ran a story headlined "Is TQM Dead?" It points out that applications for Baldridge awards—the "Oscar" of the TQM world—are down to 47 from a peak of 106 in 1991. The article cites "reengineering and disillusionment" as factors in this decline in popularity. A representative of the Deming Center for Quality Management at Columbia University, Peter Kolesar, put it this way, "A majority of companies that have gotten deeply involved in Total Quality have not made it pay off. When they don't see results quickly, they move on to something else." Frank Ingari, CEO of Shiva, commented:

> *Top management does it as a fad. You know how it goes, the same company that did quality circles is now doing reengineering. Did they ever connect those two concepts? Did they ever consider that maybe the reengineering ought to be done by the people who are responsible for the work? How much of this effort increases people's feeling of connectedness to the company?*

According to a 1994 poll cited in *Fortune* magazine, executives believe that less than one-third of TQM efforts are anything more than a "flop." The most frequently mentioned barriers to change were "employee resistance and 'dysfunctional corporate culture.'" In other words, TQM (like reeingineering) fails when the corporate culture leads employees to fear change.

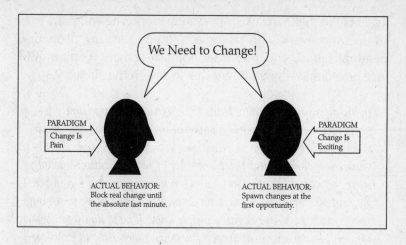

When reengineering and TQM fail, then most companies are forced into the last resort—layoffs. It's widely believed that laying off workers will automatically improve profits by cutting costs. This is not always true, however. As early as October 1993, *The Wall Street Journal* was pointing out that "many companies that slash furiously still perform poorly—and can't figure out why." One reason for this failure of downsizing was that more than half of the companies surveyed ended up refilling positions within a year of eliminating them.

However, even when "downsized" positions aren't refilled, many companies don't receive the positive results that they expected. According to downsizing expert Kenneth P. De Meuse of the University of Wisconsin, quoted in the same article, profits can decline faster after layoffs than before, "Not only is a reduction in force not a quick fix, as many companies believe, but it's most likely not a fix at all."

Layoffs generally fail when they leave in place the structures and relationships that got the company into trouble in the first place. Such layoffs diminish whatever effectiveness the company might still have by reducing the number of people available to make the existing system work. The company tries to do more work with fewer employees, creating overwork, demoralization, and pointless political activity. Former IBM vice president Willy Shih had this to say on the subject:

> In big organizations, there tends to be a leadership vacuum. Most people aren't willing to put a stake in the ground and take some risks or take some aggressive actions to change things. As the organization shrinks and there are a lot of reorganizations, people start thinking: "Oh my God, what's my next job? Am I going to get laid off?" You find inordinate amounts of time being spent on reorganization. Why? Because people know how to do those. People don't know how to approach the much more difficult problem of getting sales and revenue up or getting costs down.

Nowhere was this problem more obvious than in the way that Honeywell Information Systems, one of the traditional mainframe vendors, downsized in the 1980s.

Case Study:
Downsizing at Honeywell Information Systems

One of the first large computer companies to undergo a debilitating downsize was Honeywell Information Systems (HIS), a company that paved the way for the decline and fall of the minicomputer and mainframe vendors. Most people don't remember it today, but in 1982 HIS was the third largest computer company in the United States. It was an extraordinarily innovative company that virtually invented the minicomputer, manufactured highly reliable hardware, and had developed a multi-user operating system that was the prototype of today's popular and successful UNIX. The story of HIS is a story of a decline from industry leadership into obscurity, and the mere fact that few remember how important HIS was at one time only serves to emphasize that dramatic nature of the company's decline.

HIS is an object lesson for any company that thinks that great technology can overcome a traditional business culture. HIS, like many corporations today, was run by professional managers, few of whom really understood the products that the company was making and selling. Like many traditional firms, HIS had a Byzantine bureaucracy, lengthy chains of command, and the essential conservatism that comes along with the notion that change is inherently painful. Nevertheless, HIS was doing well in the early 1980s, selling computers in numbers that made the professional managers in the boardroom very happy indeed.

By 1988, however, HIS was on its last legs, the victim of the same market forces that we've been discussing throughout this book. Low-cost personal computers were replacing high-cost minicomputers and mainframes. The radical drop in the cost of computing power made it impossible to sell the big machines at the same inflated prices as before. Consequently, demand for HIS's mainframe products was declining rapidly.

Why didn't HIS leverage its financial power and installed base to tap the increasingly lucrative market for personal computers? The answer is that HIS, like most traditional companies, had a deep-seated fear of change. The market for personal computers was completely different from the market for mainframes. The machines were manufactured differently, shipped differently, sold differently, and supported differently. To be successful in this market, HIS would have had to remake itself, something that the managers at the top were unable to accomplish. HIS did make a deal with an off-brand manufacturer of personal computers to distribute its products, but HIS simply wasn't set up to take advantage of the new trends.

For HIS to have succeeded in the personal computer business, it would have had to change its manufacturing processes so that it could make its own PCs cost-effectively. Further, it would have had to establish relationships with dealers and distributors that sold PCs, and change its policies around pricing and support. In a company structure like Honeywell's, radical changes such as these would have taken years. They would have had to evolve slowly, with checks and balances, reviews, and approvals.

Regardless of its fear, HIS's management finally had change thrust on them in its least palatable form. Its financial position weakened to the degree that it could remain profitable only it if reduced headcount. Thus, the HIS strategy was to protect the status quo for as long as possible.

The first series of layoffs, begun in 1986, took the form of voluntary retirements. The idea was to get the most senior—and the highest paid—workers to leave the company voluntarily. The retirement packages included a generous severance known as the "golden handshake." As a result of this offer, many of the brightest and most experienced people left the company.

The second series of layoffs expanded the voluntary retirements to younger employees. As with the previous round of layoffs, Honeywell offered a generous severance package to those who were willing to leave, regardless of their role and contribution to the company. As you might expect, the people to accept this offer were those with the most up-to-date skills and the best connections in the industry. One former Honeywell employee put it this way:

The more things changed, the more they stayed the same. The people who stayed were the ones who didn't have the skills to get a better job somewhere else. It was like an IQ test: if you were smart enough to get another job, Honeywell would pay you to take it.

Why would HIS strip the company of experience and talent just when it needed them most? These half-measures created the appearance of change—of movement toward profitabil-ity—without actually requiring anything to change.

Voluntary layoffs weren't sufficient, however. Profits kept dropping as demand for HIS's machines plummeted. Top management could see no other recourse than to launch a se-ries of across-the-board layoffs. These layoffs weren't volun-tary, but they were calculated to make as little impact as possible on Honeywell's underlying structure and mecha-nisms of control. The across-the-board layoffs left the current system in place, but with fewer people. And unsurprisingly, each successive layoff further diminished HIS's effectiveness because it was trying to do the same amount of work and the same kind of work, but with fewer and fewer people.

This constant dribbling away of the company's lifeblood left the remaining employees in a state of constant fear, always waiting for the other shoe to drop. Innovation ground to a complete halt. As the layoffs continued, it became clear that only the politically savvy were surviving the carnage, and in-stead of focusing on turning the company around, employees spent their time and effort jockeying for a "safe" position. By 1990, Honeywell was staffed by confused employees wander-ing the halls like ghosts, waiting in misery for the pink slip (Figure 6.1).

Eventually, Honeywell sold its computer business to Groupe Bull, a French company heavily subsidized by the French gov-ernment. Today, HIS does little more than sell upgrades to the creaky old mainframes and minicomputers that it built and sold a decade ago. Honeywell was not the only traditional computer vendor to fall into this kind of a downward spiral. Unisys, Control Data, Wang, and Data General, to name a few, suffered from the same kind of debilitating layoffs.

Rather than seeing change as something painful, the Silicon Valley business culture embraces it, seeing it as a vehicle for future growth. Carol Bartz, CEO of AutoDesk, commented on this tendency to see change as both positive and inevitable:

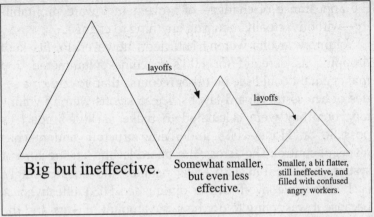

FIGURE 6.1   *The Downsizing of Honeywell Information Systems*

Change management is the toughest thing going these days. It's difficult to reward your organization for stepping out and making the bold move, even if they're wrong. But, remember, any action is better than no action in this industry. I think that the measurement system and the reward system recognizes that, a lot of times, there is no right or wrong answer.

Silicon Valley-style leaders encourage their organizations to embrace changes as positive element of their daily work environment.

The Change = Growth mindset allows individuals to remain flexible at all levels of operation. This makes organizations much more robust, able to run rings around the hidebound organizations of the industrial age, as shown in Table 6.1.

Implementation Strategies

To illustrate the Change = Growth mindset, we'll examine the four strategies that companies with Silicon Valley cultures

···

TABLE 6.1
COMPARISON OF PAIN AND GROWTH MINDSET

···

CHANGE = PAIN

• *Product Development.* Products are developed slowly, with laborious checkpoints and approvals. Products flow out the pipe slowly, if at all.

• *Reorganizing.* Reorganizing gives the appearance of change without really changing anything. Executives play musical chairs while the corporation falters.

• *Downsizing.* By trying to avoid the pain of change, management avoids downsizing until the company is too weak to survive the operation. The layoffs are drawn out over months or even years.

CHANGE = GROWTH

• *Product Development.* Products are prototyped and developed with great speed. Manufacturing expects changes based on new market conditions and helps with the design process to ensure timely delivery.

• *Reorganizing.* Organizational boundaries are flexible, so reorganizations are uncommon. People join product and service teams that form and disband as needed to get particular tasks done.

• *Downsizing.* Management plans ahead for possible market downturns. If the worst happens, management recognizes failure and quickly makes the cuts that are needed to bring the company back to long-term profitability.

···

implement to help employees embrace change as in inevitable source of renewal and growth. These strategies are:

• *Have long-term vision, short-term plans.*
• *Keep jobs fluid and flexible.*
• *Make decisions quickly and broadly.*
• *Hope for the best, prepare for the worst.*

STRATEGY 17: HAVE LONG-TERM VISION, SHORT-TERM PLANS

While the Silicon Valley companies motivate with a long-term vision (as discussed in the previous chapter) they don't believe in building long-term plans for each and every step along the way to achieving that vision. Simply put, in the fast-moving markets of the Information Age, it's foolhardy to do so. Instead, managers in Silicon Valley companies plan in relatively short time frames, often less than a year.

There's nothing inherently wrong with long-range planning, as long as it's directed at markets and opportunities that are stable enough to warrant such commitments. But when markets shift too quickly to nail down, long-range planning can inhibit company growth. Carol Bartz, CEO of AutoDesk, commented:

You can sit and ponder forever and get lost in what I call "technology purgatory." People do nothing or do something, but too little and too late. If you've only got seven- to twelve-month product lifecycles and you spend six months making a decision, you've missed your window.

Detailed long-range planning is particularly risky when it results in a rigid set of processes for managing changes. The plan, and executing to the plan become more important than satisfying customers or getting products out the door.

This means measuring what's going on today in the context of the long term vision, says SOFTBANK CEO Masayoshi Son:

On a day-to-day basis, we use what we call the "1000 marks," which is a way to analyze our business and products from at least 1000 angles. Then we make graphs of our progress and position. In the longer term, we have a 300-year corporate plan which, through abstract, helps set the stage for everything else inside the company. In this context, strategies, philosophies and vision are more important than specific numbers, actions and targets.

By contrast, Xerox is one company that has suffered from overplanning. The company, although it has an enviable reputation for developing innovative products, is also known for its inability to bring them to market. For example, Xerox pioneered the laser printer, PC networking, and even the graphical user interfaces that make personal computers so easy to use. Other companies, however, have reaped much of the benefits of Xerox's creativity, simply because Xerox suffers from the typical Industrial Age paranoia about change. Computer industry guru Jonathan Seybold commented:

Xerox had a perennial set of problems. It spends a year or more studying the requirements for a new product. This information is then passed to development, which beings a slow process of bringing the product to market. It has a five-year development cycle, much too slow for such a competitive market. On top of that, if marketing tries to change something along the way, development starts the clock again at the beginning.

Rather than following Xerox's model, Silicon Valley-style companies implement short-term plans that can be adjusted at a moment's notice to account for shifts in the marketplace. In general, the market for high-tech products is so volatile and competitive that there simply isn't time to ponder all the alternatives before making a decision. People must have a high level of personal and professional flexibility to tolerate the pressure of making frequent and potentially high-risk decisions. Carol Bartz explained:

I expect to be able to sit down with a manager and have a big "what-if" conversation—this could happen, that could happen. If people can't have that kind of discussion, they're going to be hard pressed to manage in this industry. If people need to really ponder and don't want to express an opinion, then it's harder for me to deal with them.

Strategy 18: Keep Jobs Fluid and Flexible

For an organization to be capable of reacting quickly to changes, everybody has to be flexible about job assignments and roles. In the traditional company, job roles and responsibilities are rigid, written down in job descriptions. Often, in these companies, when change is imminent, the first step management takes is to rewrite job descriptions. When market conditions shift, this rather mechanistic approach is usually ineffectual. Case in point was a company that went through a major reorganization every six months, in an effort to respond to a rapidly changing market. Each restructuring included writing detailed job descriptions, defining precise reporting relationships, and assigning goals and objectives for every group. By the time everyone had adjusted to the new hierarchy, the market caused the company to reevaluate it all again.

Effective managers don't apply such snail's-pace tactics to coping with market changes. There just isn't enough time. Bill Campbell, CEO of Intuit, put it this way:

At Claris, where I was CEO, we didn't reorganize for four years. And we grew substantially during that period, from ground zero to 100 people. Everyone worked together—that was our main principle. People think that you have to reorganize in order to adapt to new markets. They think you have to formally optimize to every little change in the marketplace. But that's bullshit. It makes more sense to leave the organization the way it is. Instead of reorganizing, make sure that management is managing people.

Get things done! Don't sit there trying to figure out new ways to organize!

Rather than concentrating on roles and responsibilities, managers should encourage the organization to be flexible, to do whatever it take to get the job done. Staff should be able to move from role to role as required, rather than be handcuffed to an outdated job description.

Inside Silicon Valley-style organizations, employees are constantly forming and reforming into teams that accomplish the task at hand. Complicated political struggles over who's in what box on the organization chart are unusual. Employees know that everything will be different in a few weeks anyway, so they simply buckle down and do what needs to be done at the moment. Sally Narodick, former CEO of Edmark, commented:

> *In today's marketplace, you must be able to move very fast and combine the creative talents of many diverse groups of people. You have to be very fluid and not hierarchical. Organizational structures and the job descriptions are constantly in flux. Formerly, we believed that a well-run company had structures and job descriptions clearly defined and written down. I still sometimes feel vaguely guilty that my company doesn't have that, when in fact, it's a strength that we don't have job descriptions and structures. A person's value is not defined by where in the hierarchy he or she is or whether he or she has a window office. People are defined by the creative talent that they bring to a project.*

Flexible work hours, too, are important when people must constantly cope with changing conditions. Today's workers have to stay on top of myriad information sources from all over the world. This requires that they be able to adjust their work hours to meet the needs of an international community. Software venture capitalist Ann Winblad told me:

There are very few jobs in this industry that are 9 to 5. Strap into your desk in the morning and just react to what you have to do that day. It probably takes most of that day. Add a few meetings to do some early planning, and then your phone system shuts down at 5 and you can get some work done for a couple hours. I would guess that probably the majority of people in this industry work from 9 to 7, that people on average put in 50-, not 40-, hour weeks. That is a fact of life here in this business. There are just so many opportunities and so many challenges that it does take up a lot of time to deal with them.

As you can see, work in Silicon Valley-style organizations has a very different rhythm, and it demands great personal flexibility. In the Industrial Age, you went to work in the morning and left in the late afternoon. You did this Monday to Friday, like clockwork, except for holidays and vacations.

That's not how it works in Silicon Valley. Their organizations tend to alternate between periods of crunch—where lots has to get done—and periods of slack—where nothing seems to be happening. During the crunch, the organization goes full bore, with people working around the clock to see that the deadline's reached. Afterward, however, they expect a period of slack, where it's considered perfectly appropriate to take some "comp time" and goof off. I worked for one organization where the programmers had the habit of taking the afternoon off and going to the cinema together whenever a new *Star Trek* movie came out. Another time I had to reschedule a meeting with Lotus Development Company's marketing group because they had all decided to attend a baseball game in the middle of the work week.

Flexibility also means letting go of the idea that everybody has to be at work at the same time. Employees generally come and go as they please. Because they're goaled on getting things done—not on warming their seats—they're free to be flexible about when they come into the office.

STRATEGY 19: MAKE DECISIONS QUICKLY AND BROADLY

A day-to-day commitment to embracing change means that companies must be able to make decisions quickly to take advantage of new opportunities. Traditionally, decision making has been a long, drawn-out affair while information is gathered, distributed, pondered, digested, and commented on. This method certainly worked in other times and other industries, but today, it's suicide. Ann Winblad commented:

> At companies such as General Electric, the methodology required that you write down your strategic assumptions in five or six areas. Then you had monthly or quarterly management reviews where you examined those strategic assumption sets again to see if they were still valid. Today, however, if you wait until once a quarter to review strategic assumptions, you could be out of business.

Decisiveness means processing information quickly, thinking creatively, pressing to a conclusion, and then acting promptly. Decisiveness also means keeping people involved in the decision-making process. Effective leaders believe that the people who are going to be affected by a decision, or implement a project that results from a decision, have the right to influence that decision. Organizations with Silicon Valley cultures still use debate and discussion prior to making a decision, but this process is not permitted to halt progress. Jonathan Seybold commented:

The way to get things done is to get consensus among the people who will do the work. The Quakers have a concept called "the sense of the meeting." There are no leaders, per se, and there's never a vote taken. After a discussion of the issues, somebody will say, "I think that the sense of the meeting is . . ." If anyone disagrees with that statement, discussion continues until a consensus is reached. Of course, there are times when I, as a manager, must make a decision that's not acceptable to everybody. However, more often than not, the "sense of the meeting" works quite well. A collective decision makes sense in most cases. Rarely do I go into a meeting with the intent to "sell" them something or with preformed opinions. If you approach people with the idea that they are responsible for making the decision, they more readily accept the process and the results of the process.

Decisiveness also means resisting the temptation to fix blame when a decision proves to be the wrong one. Effective high tech managers know that making decisions so quickly means that some of them are bound to be wrong. Safi Qureshey, Chairman Emeritus of AST Research, explained why:

I have learned that there is no perfect solution to any business challenge. There are many ways to reach any destination. And, if you are 80 percent, 85 percent, 90 percent right, your hit rate is very good. We cannot wait for the perfect data to flow in and the perfect analysis to be done. The market doesn't behave this way.

STRATEGY 20: HOPE FOR THE BEST, PREPARE FOR THE WORST

Since this quick decision making doesn't always result in success, organizations can run into problems, especially when they're competing against other Silicon Valley-style organizations. When confronted with change that is painful—such as downsizing—they approach it without fear. Mitchell Kertzman, CEO of Sybase, commented:

> *People in any company need to know that layoffs can happen. The job of management is to try to avoid it, but when it is necessary, make certain that it doesn't damage the company beyond repair. You've got to look at every person you hire as a person you might have to lay off. Now we're one of the most successful companies in the business, but we still have to be aware of the downside. We've had an up-and-down history, and I've had to lay people off, as have the other officers in this company. It gives you a sense of how to do it right, once you've gone through it once or twice. What's most important is for the company to recover and reestablish momentum as quickly as possible. Incremental cutbacks are a bad thing.*

And because these companies aren't frightened of change, they prepare for it from the start. They build their companies with the full knowledge that layoffs might happen. They hope for the best but prepare for the worst. There are three primary ways to prepare for the possibility of layoffs, even while they strengthen the viability of their organizations.

First, as already noted, look at every person you hire as somebody who might need to be laid off. This means caring about the financial status of the individual who's being hired and making certain that he or she could find employment elsewhere. In most cases, this means hiring the very best people, who, by the nature of their talents and abilities, are the most likely to be able to find other employment in the future.

Second, Silicon Valley-style companies tend to hire the minimum number of people required to do a job. This may seem obvious, but it's often ignored at companies where a Business = Battlefield mindset encourages managers to build armies and empires. Managers must refuse to gauge their success on the number of people who work for them.

Finally, Silicon Valley-style companies organize into relatively small, autonomous teams, as we discussed earlier. The product-centered, small-team organizational structure keeps employees and management aware of profitability issues, and creates an early warning system that prompts management to take remedial action before the failure of a particular product causes an undue amount of damage to the corporation at large. Such remedial actions might include shifting resources to get the product back on track, or shifting resources away from the product to ensure greater profitability. This also helps management to cut its losses more quickly and cleanly, rather than causing turmoil throughout the entire organization.

While downsizing is never pleasant, a positive attitude toward change helps companies do what needs to be done, when it needs to be done. By embracing change, the corporate culture of Silicon Valley protects their companies, at least to some degree, from the downswings that are part of any dynamic market.

Change Is Growth, Not Pain

How Evolved Is Your Organization?

The following quiz will help you to assess to how your organization views change and thus, by extension, how well it will be able to adapt to new market conditions:

• •

The Following Is True . . .

	Always	Frequently	Sometimes	Seldom	Never
1. Our executives hire management consultants with MBAs.	___	___	___	___	___
2. I do a variety of different tasks inside my job.	___	___	___	___	___
3. Risk is a "four-letter word" inside our organization.	___	___	___	___	___
4. My work changes completely every year or so.	___	___	___	___	___
5. Things always seem to go from bad to worse.	___	___	___	___	___
6. We know exactly what we need to do this fiscal quarter.	___	___	___	___	___
7. We spend many hours building long range plans.	___	___	___	___	___
8. We're ready for anything, even a downsize, God forbid.	___	___	___	___	___
9. You often hear "that's not my job" in this place.	___	___	___	___	___
10. Everybody pitches in when something unexpected happens.	___	___	___	___	___

• •

Scoring:

For all odd-numbered statements, score:

Always	1
Frequently	2
Sometimes	3
Seldom	4
Never	5

For all even-numbered statements, score:

Always	5
Frequently	4
Sometimes	3
Seldom	2
Never	1

If your score is 10–20: Your organization is terrified by the idea of change. People try to do the things that made your organization successful in the past, even when they clearly aren't working any longer. Corporate politics have become a way of life.

If your score is 21–35: Your organization is average. Sometimes your organization is flexible but often it seems too rigid and too stilted to take advantage of opportunities. Most people feel uncomfortable with new ideas and may take weeks or months to act upon them.

If your score is 36–50: Your organization is close to the Silicon Valley ideal. People actually enjoy it when their jobs change and when new opportunities arise. Little time is wasted on arguing about who's supposed to do what. You adapt quickly to new circumstances.

Points to Ponder

In order to create leverage for change, write out the answers to the following questions:

- How do you personally react to change? Do you like changes in your life? Are you committed to your own personal growth?

  _____

  _____

  _____

  _____

- How quickly do decisions get made in your organization? Can people reach agreement quickly or is there a long period of deliberation and negotiation? Are quick decisions made only when a manager decides what to do without consulting with employees? What would people in your organization have to believe in order to speed the decision-making process?

  _____

  _____

  _____

  _____

- Do you have a collection of long-range plans filed away in your desk somewhere? If so, how accurate are the plans you made a year ago? Two years ago? Five years ago? How much time did the long-range planning consume? Were the plans useful for guiding day-to-day activities or were they simply needed to get funding?

  _____

  _____

  _____

  _____

- Has your organization had a layoff lately? If so, do you feel that it was handled well? Was there turmoil and lingering pain? What could you do, today, to make certain that a layoff isn't necessary in the future? And how could you prepare for such a layoff at the same time?

  _____

  _____

  _____

  _____

Key No. 7

······································

COMPUTERS ARE SERVANTS, NOT MASTERS

······································

The Silicon Valley Mindset: Computers = Servants

Not surprisingly, companies with Silicon Valley business cultures have a very positive view of the technology that they design, manufacture, and support. They see technologies like word processing, spreadsheets, electronic mail and electronic commerce not just as vehicles for greater productivity and profitability, but as ways to create a work environment that's more healthy and humane. Former Lotus CEO Jim Manzi commented on this:

> *The nature of modern office technology challenges the fundamental power associations in the organization, because information that used to be the source of people's power is now shareable—and it should be shared. The greatest challenge is to evoke the idea that information sharing is better than information hoarding. Information sharing makes for better products, better customer service, better employee morale, and so forth. It is a fundamental challenge to basic hierarchical, command-and-control, power-oriented thinking that has characterized organizations for 2,000 years.*

This view of office technology dates from around 1970, when an influential book titled *The Office of the Future,* written

199

by computer scientists Uhlig, Farber, and Bair, described a number of advanced office technologies that were under development in academic laboratories. The book was enthusiastic about the effect that this new technology would have on the business world. According to the authors, it would provide "overwhelming advantages" and have a "very positive impact." It was predicted that people would make fewer errors and thus produce higher quality work. The book went on to anticipate an acceleration in critical business processes, more flexible work hours, and an increase in the availability of important information, all of which would result in greater job satisfaction.

The new few years saw the technological predictions of *The Office of the Future* turn into a commercial reality. By 1980, most of the traditional mainframe and minicomputer vendors had corporatewide word processing, electronic mail and so forth, and were beginning to hawk these products to their customers.

The microprocessor revolution then made office technology available on low-cost Intel-based desktops and servers. At the same time, the U.S. government began developing the Arpanet, the network that eventually grew into today's Internet. Today, that "office of the future" is a day-to-day reality.

Companies with Silicon Valley cultures tend to embrace this new technology and believe that it makes their lives better. They see office technology as a way to reduce busywork, make individuals more powerful, share information and make work hours more flexible. In other words, they view technology as the ultimate servant. Microsoft's Bill Gates put it best:

> *I predict that, by 2005, the world will be your office—and your marketplace. In this new business environment, managers will no longer be able to use information as a means to control employees; in fact, this old-style manager is already becoming extinct as organizations flatten, and empowered employee workgroups become common in the many reengineered organizations of the 1990s.*

The Traditional Mindset: Computers = Masters

This notion—that office technology will make the workplace both more productive and more humane—is a relatively recent idea. Forty years ago it was assumed that office automation would parallel factory automation. Under this way of thinking, office workers would become increasingly unnecessary as computers and robots took over the function of running the office. Office workers would, according to this theory, become the slaves of the computers, adapting their lives and circumstances to the needs of the all-powerful machines.

This vision of automation reached its apotheosis in movies like *2001—A Space Odyssey*, where the malevolent HAL9000 computer takes over a spaceship, or in the science fiction potboiler *Collosus—The Forbin Project*, where two massive computers, one in the United States and the other in the U.S.S.R. conspire to take over the world. At the time these films were made there was a great deal of computer phobia inside society at large, as well as a deep skepticism towards the people who built and supported computer technology. I had a friend who, in the late 1970s, worked as a computer programmer for Xerox. He used to tell women he wanted to date that he "fixed copiers," because if he told a prospective partner what he really did, he risked being ostracized.

Today, of course, such notions seem antiquated, mostly because of the personal computer. The PC humanized and democratized computers by putting them into the hands of nearly everyone. The power that once belonged only to gigantic corporations was now sitting on millions of desks and inside millions of homes. Computers have ceased to be frightening to most people.

The influx of PCs into the workplace and the resulting change in perception, however, was not an automatic process. Many corporations fought the introduction of PCs, seeing them as a threat to the ability of top management to control the corporation (i.e., Management = Control). It was thought unwise to put that much power in the hands of regular employees who, after all, were clearly not wise enough to use it intelligently (i.e., Employee = Child).

That attitude still exists inside many traditional corporations. There is, however, a darker side to the revolution. While companies with Silicon Valley cultures see this explosion of office technology as positive, many of the workers inside highly-automated corporations with traditional business cultures see the notion that computers liberate as something of a sick joke.

For example, as part of a research project, Harvard's Shoshana Zuboff asked a group of insurance workers what they thought of their new work experience in the automated office. Here's how one of them described it: "No talking, no looking, no walking. I have a cork in my mouth, blinders for my eyes, chains on my arms. With the radiation I have lost my hair. The only way you can make your production goals is to give up your freedom."

In this case, the management of the corporation in question had used computers, not to liberate, but to further dehumanize the work experience. Workers, who before automation were in frequent contact with one another, were put into separate cubicles and forbidden all social contact. Their productivity was now measured, not by their ability to work as part of a team, but by the number of screens that they could process during a work day. In short, management had used computer power to make these employees the slaves of the computer system.

This kind of computing strategy—common inside traditional organizations—is supposed to make them more productive. The net result, however, is often to create new problems.

For example, have you ever called a big insurance company, or big telephone company with an unusual problem, only to have the representative put you on hold, often for ten or fifteen minutes? The person you called is handling other customer requests, simple ones that don't require extra effort, whose requests fit into the pre-programmed "screens" on the representative's computer. Because your question requires extra effort, you're being put on hold until there are fewer calls. If you hang up, so much the better, because the representative is being goaled on how many customers he or she can handle each day. In some cases, the representative may actually hang up, just to get you off the line. After all, you, with your unusual request, represent an impediment to a positive productivity report. Your unusual request might even mean less money for the representative at the end of the month.

Traditional companies that "manage by the numbers" see nothing wrong in this scenario, despite the fact that such behavior leaves a foul taste in the mouth of any customer or potential customer who is forced to deal with it. I, personally, have changed insurance companies twice because I found out that "customer service" representatives were being goaled on the number of calls handled per hour by each representative. I simply got to the point where I couldn't stand the rudeness any longer.

The notion that computers should be running the show isn't limited to clerical work and telephone answering. As computers have become more common in the workplace, the Computer = Master mindset is driving companies to treat professionals in ways that are just as dehumanizing and, ultimately, just as counter-productive.

As originally defined, the office of the future was supposed to help employees to improve their lives. Workers would be able to set up home offices from which they would telecommute, performing work at home that before would have been conducted at the office. This was supposed to make it possible for parents to be closer to their families, reduce the time wasted on commuting, and even improve the environment by reducing automobile emissions.

The idea of telecommuting has been expanded to include mobile computing, a combination of technologies—notebook computers, voice mail, cellular phones—that allow a worker to transact business virtually anywhere. This concept has recently emerged in a series of television commercials from AT&T. In one of these commercials, a man sends a fax while sunning himself on a deserted beach. In another advertisement, a woman "tucks in" her baby using a two-way video phone at an airport.

Telecommuting and mobile computing, however, have opened a Pandora's box inside traditional companies. Studies reveal that the most common use of telecommuting is for workers to continue working at home after putting in a full day at the office. Similarly, mobile computing makes it possible for employees to work around the clock. Because it's possible to work all the time, many professionals feel that they must work around the clock, just to remain competitive. As a result, workers in America now "work on average 164 hours longer a year now than they did in 1970, before computers came on the scene," according to Harvard economist Juliet Schor. At the same time, the work is becoming less satisfying. A common complaint in automated offices is that work there lacks person-to-person contact that adds richness to the work experience according to the *National Productivity Review* ("Avoiding the Technology Traps in Global Business," Summer, 1991, p. 395).

In some companies, managers put subtle (and not too subtle) pressures on salaried workers to work extremely long hours. To make matters worse, some corporations are using computers to become increasingly intrusive into their employee's work habits. Electronic performance monitoring of clerical workers is now common in many high-volumn businesses. This technology lets management view and analyze the quantity of work that each person on the computer system performs.

Electronic performance monitoring is just the tip of the iceberg. Some organizations are beginning to monitor their employees' electronic mail traffic. Other companies are testing key card technology that allows management to track the exact location of employees inside a building. Japanese firms are now offering technology that could make it possible to track down a worker anywhere in the world.

This kind of technology could easily be used to apply additional pressure upon employees to work longer and longer hours. The only regulation of such intrusive practices is a "system of free market and common law mechanisms that fails to protect workers from abusive practices," according to the *Harvard Law Review* ("Addressing the New Hazards of the High Technology Workplace," *104*(8), 1991, p. 1898).

All of this in the name of higher productivity. Ironically, there's little documented correlation between long work hours and productivity. For example, workers in Germany consistently out-produce workers in the United Kingdom, even though the average German worker puts in ninety hours less per year than the average United Kingdom worker. Common sense tells us that tired, stressed-out people make mistakes and poor decisions. Working longer is not the same as working smarter.

Furthermore, sick workers are not productive workers. The rise of the automated office has been matched by a sharp increase in work-related health problems including headaches, muscle fatigue, blurred vision, repetitive stress injuries, carpal tunnel syndrome, tendinitis and lower back pain. In addition to lost hours, sick times, work slowdowns, health problems contribute to today's steady increase in worker's compensation losses, further eroding productivity and job satisfaction.

I once paid a visit to the marketing department of a company that had just installed a workflow system. (Workflow is an office technology that lets a manager track the different steps of a multistep project.) It was a small company and the marketing department consisted of two people—a manager and a marketing specialist. The marketing manager waxed eloquent about how wonderful the workflow system was. "The great thing about it," he told me, "is that anytime I think of what needs to be done, I can just enter it into the system and I know that my marketing department will see that it gets done." While he was telling me this, I happened to glance up at the marketing specialist who was sitting behind the manager. She rolled her eyes, grimaced, and raised her hands as if she were going to strangle him. The manager noticed that my attention was distracted and turned around, but by the time he could see the specialist, a blank expression had returned to her face. Later, I asked the marketing specialist what was going on. She told me, "Ever since we got that workflow system, he's been driving me out of my mind with trivial action items."

Companies that believe in the Management = Control mindset will inevitably be drawn to the Computers = Master mindset, with the managers in control of the computers. In this case, technology can become an extraordinary burden, a vehicle for previously unattainable levels of micromanagement.

And it's not over yet. A technology that's just around the corner is two-way video conferencing, right on your personal computer. You'll be able to call up other people and actually see them on the screen and they'll see you. If this sounds familiar, it might be because you remember the old Jetson's television cartoon show. On the show, the hero, George Jetson, works in front of a screen on which his boss—an overbearing twerp—appears periodically to either spy on George or perhaps to yell at him to "GET BACK TO WORK!" Silly as the cartoon seemed at the time, it carries an important warning, because the more technology we introduce into the workplace, the more we have the potential to empower over-bearing bosses and bureaucrats, to the ultimate detriment of both the individual and the team.

Case Study: The Early Adopters of Electronic Mail

History has shown that combining advanced technology and traditional business culture results in a highly toxic mixture. That makes sense, if you think about it, because the traditional business culture evolved during a time when women weren't allowed to vote, slavery was legal, mass media was a broadside newspaper, and long-distance communication was a letter on a sailing ship. As a result, traditional corporations—even those who make high-tech products—can be saddled with a business culture that belongs to a prior stage in our technological development.

This became clear to me in 1992 at an office automation conference in Boston. On the discussion panel were representatives of IBM, Digital, and Wang—the three traditional industry leaders in corporate-wide electronic mail. All three had been selling electronic mail for over a decade. Although PC-based mail products like cc:Mail from Lotus were eating away at the edges of their market share, all three companies had solid customer bases.

The guys on the panel were carefully dressed in impeccable wool suits, as alike as three peas in a pod. Their presentations were the same as well. All three agreed that electronic mail would inevitably make companies more productive. The promises were familiar:

"Executives will be better informed."

"Managers and employees will communicate more quickly."

"Tedious paperwork will be eliminated."

"Vast sums of money will be saved."

The audience consisted mostly of conservatively dressed computer professionals who had built their careers selling the benefits of IBM, Digital, and Wang equipment inside their own companies. Presently, the session moderator asked for questions from the floor. A few audience members raised their hands, seeking clarification of minor points. Then silence—the respectful kind of silence that often happens at the end of a successful, if uncontroversial, conference session. The moderator was about to close the session, when a young man in the back of the room raised his hand. I have to admit that he looked a little out of place at the conference, for he was dressed in jeans, T-shirt and high-top tennis shoes:

"I have a couple of questions," he said.

The man from IBM smiled indulgently: "Let's have them, son."

"Do you use your own products?"

The man from IBM glanced at his fellow panel members, who nodded. "Why, of course. We wouldn't ask our customers to buy something that we didn't use ourselves."

The young man in the audience scratched his head. "Well, if electronic mail is so great and can make employees so productive and give them such a competitive advantage, how come IBM, Digital, and Wang revenues are all going down the toilet?" Remember, this was in 1992, and all three companies were in deep financial trouble.

The guys on the panel looked as if they had been slapped in the face. The audience shuffled in discomfort. After all, nobody likes to hear that the emperor has no clothes, especially if you've been buying from the same tailor. The Digital guy muttered a lame joke about becoming "unintentionally nonprofit," but it was too late. The atmosphere of self-satisfied chumminess had disappeared. When the moderator closed the session, people left the room muttering to themselves and avoiding the young man who had asked the offending question.

And yet, the question was a valid one. For years, the traditional mainframe and minicomputer vendors had been claiming that electronic mail made companies more competitive, better able to adapt to rapid market changes. And they had been using their own technology for years. Unfortunately, technology by itself isn't enough.

Unless the corporate culture is ready for the new technology, productivity gains are likely to prove elusive. In fact, the combination of electronic mail and traditional business culture, far from making traditional businesses more effective, can even make them less effective than before. Let's look at Wang Laboratories first. Wang was an early pioneer in electronic mail, both in selling it to customers and using it in-house.

Despite Wang's long experience with the technology, however, the organization didn't use electronic mail very effectively, according to former Wang employee Ann Palermo, who was recently the groupware vice president at International Data Corporation, one of the largest computer market research firms in the world:

I don't know if electronic mail makes companies more efficient. It's really just an alternative means of communicating. For example, at Wang, there was a formal protocol for electronic mail. If you sent something a few levels above your own, you had to copy everybody in between. There wasn't the free flow of information that everybody anticipates with electronic mail. It was very political. You had to be careful how you worded things and what kinds of issues you raised. It was like memo writing, only quicker. It created a lot more fire drills, a lot more panics about one thing or another—a lot of running around.

Electronic mail at (the old) Wang did make communications faster. The management, however, tried to use this improved communication to gain greater control over employee behavior. This increased the number of orders from headquarters, as well as the number of requests for status reports. Wang employees began to focus more on internal issues rather than building products that customers wanted. Wang's electronic mail system was used as a mechanism to oversee, to check on progress, to intrude on the day-to-day doings of the regular employees.

Prior to the installation of electronic mail at Wang, there was a balance—albeit an uneasy one—of power between headquarters, the engineers, marketers, and salespeople. Electronic mail put power firmly at Wang headquarters. This weakened Wang by making it *more* centralized and thus *less* able to react to market changes. While many factors were contributing to Wang's decreasing fortunes, electronic mail—rather than acting as a productivity panacea—was actually making things worse.

The danger with electronic mail is that it can create a corporate cyberspace where managers have so much immediate access to information that they want to micromanage everything. Rather than being used as a tool for coordinating activities, the electronic mail system can degenerate into a means to centralize control of an organization, thus extracting individual initiative.

In the 1980s, electronic mail became the tool IBM's corporate bureaucrats needed to guarantee that nothing was done without their prior approval. This made it increasingly difficult for the company to launch new products, while simultaneously reinforcing the status quo. A former IBM vice president had this to say about the way electronic mail was used at IBM:

E-mail was designed to facilitate, but what it did was make people prisoners of the system. For the sake of the efficiency, a lot of procedures have been automated. But people seldom ask: "Why am I doing this procedure?" Procedures that are automated become almost impossible to change. They think they're so clever for automating all this stuff but it's really an albatross around their neck.

The main peril is that the corporate bureaucracy will actually use the system to get "control" of the company. In that case, something very curious is likely to happen. Rather than using the electronic mail system to increase the speed with which the bureaucracy grants approval, the bureaucracy uses the electronic mail system to require approval for an increasing number of employee activities. Giving electronic mail to bureaucrats simply serves to empower the bureaucrats, making organizations *more* bureaucratic and therefore *less* productive. Sybase CEO Mitchell Kertzman commented:

Most organizations use electronic technologies as a modernization of their existing communication methods and human interactions, rather than using them to significantly change things.

The more powerful the technology and the greater the potential benefit, the greater the potential for abuse. With electronic mail, a well-run organization will become better run, because information will flow faster. A poorly run organization, on the other hand, will simply become even more dysfunctional.

Case in point: Digital Equipment Corporation in the late 1970s and early 1980s. According to authors Glenn Rifkin and George Harrar (in their excellent 1988 book, *The Ultimate Entrepreneur*, Contemporary Books, 1988), Digital at that time was a hotbed of internal politics, with much of the backbiting and intrigue conducted via electronic mail. According to one product line manager, "you had to read your mail *before* you went to work because they would send copies to everybody and maybe a thousand people would see some cheap shot before you even got to the office." This misuse of electronic mail put extraordinary stress on the company's key leaders. At least one manager felt obligated to wake up at 4 A.M., just to keep tabs on the political situation. According to authors Rifkin and Harrar, electronic mail became a convenient way to spread those two hallmarks of the predatory bureaucrat—"innuendo and rumor."

At Wang, IBM, and Digital, electronic mail only served to emphasize and strengthen the dysfunctional behaviors already taking place at these companies. The problem, however, wasn't the technology, but the traditional cultures of these corporations.

Effective managers in high-tech companies use office technology to strengthen their already powerful corporate cultures. They do this by using office technology to build flatter organizational structures and as a vehicle for dispersing power downward into the company. I asked former Microsoft executive vice president Mike Maples how the use of electronic mail there differed from the way it was used inside the traditional vendors such as Wang and IBM:

When you commit a high percentage of your communication to electronic mail—as we do at Microsoft—then you process a lot more transactions per day. You don't have 15-minute meetings on one-minute subjects. You have better control of your time and are more likely to hear about things that you need to know about. Electronic mail encourages, but doesn't require, a much flatter, much more democratic kind of organization. To some extent, the acceptance of that organizational change is probably one of the most important elements. I don't think electronic mail makes you do that, but it allows you to do that. If you still have a strict hierarchical organization, and you're allowed to send mail only to your boss, and your boss forwards it to his boss, and you go through the organizational disciplines and protocols that were established in the old days, then it hasn't helped you.

The lesson is this: *Technology doesn't solve problems—it accelerates behavior.* If the behavior inside a company is fundamentally productive, then chances are that technology will make it more productive. If, however, the behavior inside a company are dysfunctional, then technology will make things worse.

It must be emphasized that this is not a problem with office technology, per se. Problems occur because the technology is used in a way that's ineffective, dangerous and ultimately non-productive. Computer technology may make problems worse, but the original source of the problem is dysfunctional beliefs and business behaviors.

The impact, then—positive or negative—of technology depends on the dominant mindsets within an organization. Companies that have internalized the traditional business culture will find that technology strengthens those behaviors, detailed in Table 7.1.

Implementation Strategies

The way that a corporation uses computers deeply influences productivity. Companies that use computers to dehumanize and oppress, make themselves brittle and ineffective. Companies that use office technology effectively become "supercharged"—able to take on nearly any challenge. The way to implement the Computers = Servants mindset is to increase the quality of communication inside the organization. Thus, rather than isolating people in electronic island, office technology helps to build a stronger corporate community. There are three ways to accomplish this:

- *Use electronic mail (e-mail) to flatten management.*
- *Humanize electronic communications.*
- *Reduce information pollution.*

Let's examine each of these strategies in detail.

TABLE 7.1
COMPARISON OF MASTER AND SERVANT MINDSETS

COMPUTERS = MASTERS

- *Rigidity.* Companies use office technology to strengthen chains of command and to conduct internal political battles. The company becomes inwardly focused and increasingly paranoid of "enemies."
- *Micromanagement.* Companies use office technology to set up automated procedures that inhibit human initiative, ensuring compliance with established rules and regulations. The company becomes increasingly inflexible as power concentrates at the top. Employees become even more alienated and disconnected from the organization's goals.
- *Intrusiveness.* Companies use office technology to monitor daily activities of employees, using technology to demand unpaid overtime, calling it "professionalism." Employees resent the scrutiny and focus on "getting away with things," or become burned out and unable to make reasonable decisions.

COMPUTERS = SERVANTS

- *Flexibility.* Companies use office technology to identify new opportunities and develop businesses to exploit them, resulting in consistent and profitable growth through the rapid development of new opportunities.
- *Cohesiveness.* Companies use office technology to help people build healthy internal and external relationships, making management more accessible. Employees (even at remote sites) feel loyal and dedicated to the organization's goals. They also feel more connected to and supported by management, not smothered by it.
- *Power Dispersion.* Companies use electronic mail to disperse responsibility and authority to employee "businesses," expanding and eliminating organizational boundaries. Employees claim ownership of their projects, while communications flow more freely, enabling everyone to learn and adapt more quickly.

STRATEGY 21: USE ELECTRONIC MAIL
TO FLATTEN MANAGEMENT

Electronic mail is much more than a faster way to send memos. It is a way of implementing the kind of responsive and flexible organizations that are most likely to react productively to market conditions. Solfware venture capitalist and industry savant Ann Winblad told me:

> *At Microsoft, communication pervades the entire organization. There's no Microsoft executive or employee who doesn't travel with a notebook computer, and they're constantly checking their electronic mail. Electronic mail routes around that company at all levels. Electronic mail allows the organization to be much flatter from a communications standpoint than in the traditional company.*

Former Microsoft executive vice president Mike Maples commented that electronic mail has been a vehicle for keeping Microsoft free of the kind of political infighting that freezes many Industrial Age companies:

> *The electronic mail system has the consequences of eliminating organizational politics, which flourish when you tell one person one thing and another person something else. When you have a flat organization where everybody's in the discussion all the time, the number of "side deals" are greatly minimized. Because what somebody says is so easily copied and redistributed, people have to be much clearer and much more direct, merely because the mechanism for distribution of the information is so efficient. We try not to have competing missions or competing objectives. We try not to have one organization viewing another organization as their competition or in the way of their success. You can never have that perfect, but we work real hard at trying to "empower" the teams to do their own thing.*

The same can be true in a smaller company. For example, former Edmark CEO Sally Narodick explained how Edmark used electronic mail to keep people involved in the decision-making process:

> We make tremendous use of voice mail and e-mail, and we've invested a fair amount of time to get it up and running. It has paid for itself a thousandfold in terms of helping teams work together. There are so many things that you can do with the new technology. You can make sure everybody's briefed, or has a chance to present his or her angle of the topic into the discussion. We believe that information is power and try to make key business information available broadly. We have our own homegrown groupware that we use to share documents and files. It's the heart of what we do in our culture and how we manage. Thanks to these vehicles, almost no one goes through a hierarchical structure to talk to another person or to review things. We just chatter across all different kinds of lines to get things done, to brief people, to get input.

Another heavy user of electronic mail is Sun Microsystems. CEO Scott McNealy is so "plugged in" to his electronic mail system that he doesn't even put it aside when he's being interviewed. Here's what Scott told me when I asked him about electronic mail usage at Sun:

> We have an e-mail culture, so information is distributed immediately and massively throughout the company. For example, while you and I were talking, I just got an e-mail that told me what the stock price was today when the market closed. I had another flash this morning about IBM . . . You have so much instantaneous access. I don't have to wait for the newspaper to come out. All the stuff that I need to know just starts showing up on my e-mail. E-mail also allows us to run a flatter organization

because we can get everybody rolling in the same cadence, because the information out there is so much more clear.

Companies that manage the Silicon Valley way aren't afraid to put the power of electronic mail into the hands of all their employees. Mike Maples commented:

At Microsoft, anybody that needs to be aware of a subject anywhere in the organization is copied on the original piece of mail. This tends to short-circuit the filtering of information. You have a much faster movement of information from the time of an action to the time that everybody knows about the action. It encourages people at multiple levels to enter the debate simultaneously so you don't have to have a workgroup debate an issue, take it to the manager, debate the issue again, take it to another manager, for more debate, and filter it up the chain of command. Instead, decision making happens in real time with people at all levels in the organization.

Ideally, electronic mail becomes a vehicle for the rapid decision making that's so important to a growing, nimble organization.

STRATEGY 22: HUMANIZE ELECTRONIC COMMUNICATIONS

It's always better to give feedback in person, because feedback by its very nature is personal. Being physically close gives both of you important information that's communicated by facial expressions, gestures, body language and so forth. Being close when you're giving feedback also allows you to better assess whether or not the other person is in an emotional state to receive your feedback and act upon it.

For example, suppose you're communicating to a co-worker that his or her performance hasn't been well received. If the co-worker gets upset and angry, it's pointless to give advice. Instead, it makes much more sense to wait until the co-worker calms down and then begin working on what can be done to make the situation better. This is much easier to do in person than remotely.

Person-to-person feedback, however ideal, isn't always possible in the business world. Many organizations are dispersed around the globe, making it necessary to give and receive feedback less directly, such as with a telephone call. While telephone communication is not as "rich" as face-to-face talking, it still carries an important source of emotional information—the tonality of the voice. It also allows for the give-and-take discussion that's so essential to effective feedback.

Effective feedback becomes even more challenging inside today's highly computerized workplace, where it's not unusual to have work teams with members who live on different continents. Such workgroups often use a variety of technological marvels to move their projects along, including fax machines, voice mail, electronic mail, intranets, and groupware.

Unfortunately, this fancy technology still lacks the emotional impact of a telephone call, let alone a face-to-face discussion. Long distance feedback—especially when conducted through a written medium like electronic mail—can thus become antiseptic and unfeeling. This can, in turn, damage or destroy those precious and positive relationships—a primary source of growth and profit.

Giving effective feedback over long distances thus presents some special challenges, which are addressed by three simple rules:

1. *Always try to give negative feedback in person or (worst case) over the telephone.* Feedback is, by its very nature, emotional, because people connect it to their future, their sense of contribution, and

their ability to achieve their goals. Even the driest note from the most emotionless bureaucrat in the world is going to spark emotion in the recepient if it contains criticism. Best that you—as the giver of feedback—do what you can to make certain the emotional content is interpreted appropriately and, more importantly, results in personal growth and in improved performance. This means giving negative feedback in person whenever possible.

2. *If you must give feedback remotely, get to know the person first.* Teams that are dispersed geographically work much better together if they've met in person, and even better if they meet in person frequently. Despite all the hype surrounding the information age, there's no substitute for actually "experiencing" the people with whom you'll be working. Personal contact, when possible, promotes an atmosphere of friendship and camaraderie that easily carries over into electronic communications. If you can't meet personally, use the telephone to make a personal contact. The more that you establish a personal connection with the person you wish to influence, the more you'll be able to influence that person to do better in the future.

3. *Be twice as diplomatic and sensitive as you would be in person.* It's especially important to frame long-distance feedback in a positive way. Make a special point to praise before criticizing. Spend the time to communicate with words, what you might otherwise communicate with a helpful smile or a touch on the shoulder. The result will be fewer hurt feelings and a more positive reaction to the feedback process. In particular, don't use electronic mail to lob "grenades" at co-workers. Electronic mail can be very destructive if the communication is negative, because when messages are copied, it can bring other people into the fray.

STRATEGY 23: REDUCE INFORMATION POLLUTION

Companies that are overloaded with information can easily become overwhelmed with trivia. In this case, the flood of information puts the entire organization in thrall to the computer, unable to take action because there's too much information to make a good decision.

Information overload occurs when there's simply too much information to make a good decision. According to the Delphi Consulting Group, computers produce over one billion pages of output every day. To put this into perspective, a billion pages laid end-to-end would circle the earth over twenty times. Stacked in reams, it would tower ten times higher than Mount Everest. The amount of paper output produced in just *two seconds* would totally fill the average office, ceiling to floor.

This vast explosion of information makes it difficult to find the right information at the right time. According to Robert Half Consulting, senior executives now spend over an hour each day searching for information. This is an extraordinary figure, especially considering that most executives have entire staffs to provide them with data. Some professionals, according to time management guru Alec Mackensie ("The Time Trap," Amacom, 1990), spend approximately *ninety-four days a year* just handling paperwork.

Equally dangerous to information overload is information contamination. This occurs when inaccurate data poses as accurate data. Inaccurate information has always been a hazard. However, today's desktop technology, when poorly utilized, tends to increase rather than decrease information contamination.

For example, word processing makes it easy for writers to keep updating a document until the last minute. A misplaced keystroke, entered in haste, can delete vital information. Because word processing ensures that the document looks "professional," major errors often slip by unnoticed. Spreadsheets are even worse. One misplaced decimal point can ripple through an entire spreadsheet, making hundreds of tables, graphs and slides inaccurate. Few people who build spreadsheets bother to document or desk-check their spreadsheet programs. The result is information that's contaminated with questionable and inaccurate data.

Information contamination becomes particularly toxic when word processing and spreadsheet files are made available to multiple users on a network. With an electronic mail system, a contaminated document can spread across an organization like a virus, resulting in a series of poor business decisions. According to *InfoWorld*, a survey of IT professionals revealed that nearly 60 percent of America's largest corporations have been adversely affected by corrupted or incomplete data from personal computers, shreadsheets, and networks.

The notion that information is like money leads users to stockpile and disseminate documents without regard for accuracy or appropriateness. This increases the overall level of information pollution, impairing the ability of an organization to make good business decisions. Ironically, information pollution then results in financial loss, trading real profitability for the fool's gold of "information richness."

There are some features and characteristics of office that, if not held in check, can make the problem of information overload even worse. Keep in mind that with a single keystroke, e-mail users can send a message to a distribution list containing hundreds of recipients. When the information justifies that kind of distribution, it's great, but often employees overestimate the importance of what they have to communicate. This results in electronic junk mail that, just like its paper predecessor, clutters up the system, making it difficult and unpleasant to find the really important materials.

Fortunately, the solution to this problem isn't at all complicated and merely involves personal discipline. Companies with Silicon Valley cultures encourage employees to use office technology—especially electronic mail—responsibly, which may require setting some guidelines for proper usage. This isn't to say that management dictates a set of rules; instead, a set of guidelines emerge that help keep the flood of information under control. For example, with electronic mail, the following guidelines are in place inside most Silicon Valley organizations:

1. *Inform, don't overload.* Constantly ask yourself: "Do these people really need to know this bit of information?" Don't gain a reputation as someone who sends out lots of meaningless messages. People will start deleting your messages, unread, assuming they're not important. Far better to be the kind of person who sends electronic mail only when it's really relevant. That way your messages will get read first.

2. *Use a descriptive mail header.* A mail header is the title of the message that appears in the recipient's list of new mail. Create a header that explains briefly and clearly what the message is about. Recipients are often so swamped with mail messages that they rely on the headers to sort through them.

3. *Keep messages short and well-thought-out.* If possible, write a message that's no longer than the size of the average screen display. If you must communicate something lengthier, summarize the document in the first screen and end that first screen with "details to follow." Electronic mail messages should be written like newspaper stories: headlines first, followed by the main points, followed by the details in decreasing order of importance.

How Evolved Is Your Organization?

The following quiz will allow you to assess how well your organization is using its office technology—either to enhance or detract from overall productivity:

The Following Is True . . .

	Always	Frequently	Sometimes	Seldom	Never
1. Our company monitors our electronic mail.	___	___	___	___	___
2. We have reasonable guidelines for e-mail usage.	___	___	___	___	___
3. We're frequently expected to work unpaid overtime.	___	___	___	___	___
4. I have been able to build good relationships through e-mail.	___	___	___	___	___
5. I regularly get e-mail messages from bureaucrats.	___	___	___	___	___
6. I have control over most of my computing resources.	___	___	___	___	___
7. We use computers in order to avoid face-to-face contact.	___	___	___	___	___
8. Our management structure is flatter since we got e-mail.	___	___	___	___	___
9. People send electronic "flame-o-grams" full of hostility and rage.	___	___	___	___	___
10. E-mail messages regularly bypass layers of management.	___	___	___	___	___

Scoring:

For all odd-numbered statements, score:

Always	1
Frequently	2
Sometimes	3
Seldom	4
Never	5

For all even-numbered statements, score:

Always	5
Frequently	4
Sometimes	3
Seldom	2
Never	1

If your score is 10–20: Your organization uses computers in order to strengthen the control of management over the rest of the company. Many workers are demoralized and feel dehumanized. Managers are deluged with information that they really can't use. The executives may have stopped using e-mail altogether, merely to avoid becoming overwhelmed.

If your score is 21–35: Your organization is average. Office technology is generally effective, but there are sometimes problems that seem to damage productivity. You sometimes wonder whether you might not be better off without all the fancy gadgets, but you also know that it would be difficult to get along without them.

If your score is 36–50: Your organization is close to the Silicon Valley ideal. Office technology is used as a vehicle to create a more flexible and powerful workplace. People communicate with one another throughout the organization, increasing the speed with which decisions are made.

Points to Ponder

In order to create leverage for change, write out the answers to the following questions:

- How many hours of your day are consumed reading and answering electronic mail? Is there some way that you make this time more productive?

  _____

  _____

  _____

  _____

  _____

- What kind of business culture would your organization have if it had the most advanced technology on the planet?

  _____

  _____

  _____

  _____

- How would your management philosophy have to change in order to allow people to work remotely, without direct supervision?

  _____

  _____

  _____

  _____

- What technologies do you think will become possible in the future. How do you expect yourself and your organization to adapt to them?

_____

_____

_____

_____

_____

With all its powerful technology, Silicon Valley culture isn't for the timid. It demands a significant commitment from the people who work inside such companies. Even when the culture treats computers as servants, the fierceness of the competition may demand long hours and tight deadlines and constant change. This raises the constant specter of people becoming burnt-out and tired, even with the best of intentions. In order to avoid this, one final key is essential . . .

Key No. 8

TRANSFORM WORK INTO PLAY, NOT TOIL

••

The Silicon Valley Mindset:
Work = Play

People who work inside Silicon Valley-style companies share an extremely optimistic view of the office of the future. They practice what they preach—and sell—and thus feel confident that electronic mail, voice mail, cellular phones, and portable computers will make organizations more productive. They're predicting that the office technology of the future is destined to change the business world. Here's how Microsoft Chairman Bill Gates put it:

> *In the office of the future, intelligent applications, high-band-width networks, and innovative devices will connect people and information wherever they are—homes, cars, or public kiosks. For example, a "virtual team" of experts around the world could work together to produce a report. They could meet, pass infor-mation, documents, images, and large files back and forth—or review them together—saving the time and expense of travel. The network becomes their "virtual conference room." Smaller central offices, more cost-effective ways to train and communi-cate with employees, and greater flexibility in reaching cus-tomers, add up to a better bottom line for business. Businesses will also have greater access to global resources. This means*

getting precisely the right information and people for every job—
and increasing productivity and quality.

What's interesting about Bill's statement is the idea that it's important for technology to make it possible to put the "right" people into the right job. This reflects a deeply held belief in Silicon Valley culture that people should be doing work that they enjoy. In this new business culture, work is considered something that's supposed to be fun.

You also see this attitude reflected in Microsoft's products. For example, the installation program for the Windows 95 operating system, when describing the primary attributes of the new system, notes that "everything you do will be more fun"— as if that were an important attribute for software to have, even though the majority of Windows 95 systems are in machines that are used inside business environments. Inside companies with Silicon Valley cultures, employees tend to treat work as if it were their favorite hobby. For example, it's not unusual for employees to come into work on weekends, not just because it's expected of them, because they truly enjoy their jobs. Although there are exceptions, by and large, the employees of Silicon Valley companies look on work as something to be enjoyed rather than merely endured.

One company that encourages and expects its employees to treat work as their hobby is Microsoft. To learn about this, and other aspects of Microsoft's culture, I interviewed Mike Maples, who retired from Microsoft in mid-1995 after serving as executive vice president for worldwide products since 1988. Mike commented on how he and other Microsoft employees view their jobs:

> *I'm really lucky that my job and that my hobby are the same*
> *thing. I go home on Saturday afternoons and the thing I want to*
> *do is play with software, look at it, see what other people have*
> *done and how they've done it, and how it might be useful. If I*

were working at a bank, I'd probably go home and work on com-
puters on the weekend and in the evenings. We probably all share
a passion for the technology and the products, which makes some
of the outside activities kind of blend together. One of the things
that I enjoy reading is computer books, and so, instead of reading
about deer hunting, I'm reading about computers.

To be sure, these people work hard—very hard—but they bring a sense of joy to what they do. Take, for example, Edward McCracken, the CEO of Silicon Graphics Incorporated (SGI), the company that makes the high-powered workstations that Hollywood uses to create magic on the big screen, such as the dinosaurs that prowled through *Jurassic Park.* Edward told me:

We thrive on self-motivation. Our people work really hard and
they play really hard. We think it's important that our people
have fun working. We like to say that we have serious fun, be-
cause we produce what we think are the world's best systems.
Our employees really relate to that.

One company that carries this sense of playfulness to an ex-treme is Sun Microsystems. In addition to Sun's sponsorship of sports activities, Sun has a tradition of April Fool's jokes, gener-ally played by employees on their managers. For example, one manager at Sun discovered a replica of his office submerged in the bottom of an aquarium full of sharks. One of the co-founders, Bill Joy, found his Ferrari parked in a shallow pond, replete with a bumper sticker reading "I brake for flamingos." Even CEO Scott McNealy isn't sacrosanct. He arrived one April Fool's morning to discover that his office had been turned into a one-hole, par-four miniature golf course.

What's important here isn't the silliness of the pranks, but the underlying cultural values that make these pranks accept-able. Because the individuals leading these organizations truly believe that work is supposed to be fun, they find occasions to make it so. It's also significant that the executives are the butt of the jokes. Can you imagine Andrew Carnegie, or General Electric CEO Jack Welsh for that matter, thinking it was not only funny, but appropriate, for their employees to turn the CEO's personal office into a golf course?

The Traditional Mindset:
Work = Toil

That kind of lighthearted approach to work is virtually non-existent inside companies with traditional corporate cultures. Industrial Age attitudes toward work are so closely coupled with the traditional "puritan work ethic" that the idea of workers having fun and enjoying their jobs seems either impossible or undesirable.

A friend of mine works for Nashua Corp., a highly traditional company that manufactures photographic supplies. One day I noticed that he looked a bit crestfallen, and he explained why. He told me that Nashua had a policy, like many corporations, of "casual Fridays," where employees could wear whatever they wanted. "But now they're going back to a dress code!" He then added a few expletives illustrating his opinion of the new rules. I decided to give Nashua Corp. a call to discover the reason behind the decision. I got through to the manager of Human Resources, who explained that the senior management team felt that people were having "too much fun." It wasn't businesslike, and "we decided that it would be better for the company if we went back to our original dress code."

What is sad about this situation is that the managers at Nashua Corp. clearly believed that unless workers were miserable, then they must not be working hard enough. A sense of fun was seen as a dangerous distraction from "serious" business. Ironically, Nashua Corp. used to have a thriving business creating high-tech supplies and components. Nashua Corp.

was unable to compete with a host of other companies, many of which have Silicon Valley cultures. The hard-nosed attitude of Nashua's management, rather than making the company more productive, merely added to the company's morale problems, making it even less able to compete.

It isn't just managers who are infected with this notion that work should be difficult and painful. There are many workers whose work experience has been so negative that they scoff at the very idea that work can be enjoyable. These are the "Thank-God-It's-Friday" nine-to-fivers, who can't wait for the weekend to begin. For them, work is an obnoxious chore, to be gotten over with as soon as possible, so that they can get back to what they really enjoy. But because such people often intensely dislike or at best tolerate their jobs, they're often too tired at the day's end to do much more than plop in front of the television. And as for making their companies and teams more productive—nothing could be further from their minds.

The ideal, inside Silicon Valley culture, is to cultivate an environment where people neither work to live nor live to work, but love to work. By viewing work as a form of play, people make job satisfaction into a given. Success is not measured completely by wealth—although wealth may come—and not even by achievement—although achievement is probably assured—but by the amount of joy that they extract from all that the world has to offer, including (and especially) the work experience. Sybase CEO Mitchell Kertzman commented:

> I care a lot about the people here. It's more than just providing a flexible environment and good benefits and all those things. I try to create an environment where people can adhere to their personal high values and feel that these are consistent with the company's values and the company's goals. I believe that virtually every person knows the right thing to do in any situation. I want to create a company where that right thing to do by your value judgment as a good human being is also the right thing to do for

the company. The right thing to do and what the company wants me to do should be congruent. They should be the same.

Far from thinking that productivity comes from pushing workers to the point of misery, companies with a Silicon Valley culture embrace the notion that an enjoyable work environment makes companies more productive. The validity of this belief is clearly shown in the following case studies.

Case Study: Cabletron Battles Cisco for Market Share

Bob Levine and Craig Benson, the co-founders of Cabletron have always been the "bad boys" of the networking world. An avid musclebuilder, President/CEO Levine has been known to dress up in Rambo fatigues and thrust combat knives through basketballs in order to motivate his sales troops. Levine (who has since left the company) collects military vehicles and even owned his own tank—for a while at least—until he totaled it into a tree. Chairman/COO Benson, on the other hand, has a reputation for absolute ruthlessness, and once fired an employee who hadn't actually started his job yet, because he "hated" the guy after meeting him on a company-sponsored Sunday boat trip.

Cabletron has got a reputation for being a difficult place to work. Support people, for example, are reputedly asked to work over holidays, trying to troubleshoot customer networks. One woman actually worked 36 hours straight, without so much as a "thank-you" from top management, according to a co-worker. People feel obligated to work absurd hours because they know that they'll be fired if they don't perform. And this isn't just an empty threat. In 1990, for example, Cabletron fired fully 10 percent of its white collar workforce according to

Inc. magazine, even though the company was growing by leaps and bounds.

As you might expect in a company that had assimilated a highly militaristic attitude, the company has had problems with sexual discrimination. According to local newspaper accounts, Benson once ordered a male supervisor to fire a woman and replace her with a man. "Put a guy in (her) position," Benson allegedly said. The supervisor refused and, when he was fired, filed suit. The lawsuit, which dragged on for years, finally resulted in a $2 million award. (Cabletron maintains that Benson's intentions were misinterpreted, which is why the company pursued the case in court.)

To be fair, Cabletron officials deny that the company favors male employees, pointing out that 36 percent of the company's employees are female, but that 40 percent of the promotions last year were of female employees. However, the company does have problems retaining personnel, as shown by an exodus of executive talent in late 1996.

By all accounts, Cabletron is a very difficult environment in which to work. Cabletron's culture thrives on conflict, treating business as if it were a battle in which only one company can emerge as the winner, driving employees as if they were faceless "grunts" going off to battle. The problem with this kind of corporate culture is that it has an undeniable tendency to treat outsiders as enemies. This makes it extremely very difficult for the militaristic company to master the fine art of "co-opetition," in which one partners with one's competitors.

Cabletron's most important competitor is Cisco Systems. In contrast to Cabletron's highly militarized work environments, Cisco is an archetypal Silicon Valley company, deeply concerned with the diversity and well being of its employees. For example, Cisco spends an enormous amount of time and effort on making certain that managers and employees can communicate well with one another. Up to 40 percent of Cisco's in-house management training deals with improving communication and feedback skills, according to Beau Parnell, Cisco's director of Human Resources. This goes back to the days of Cisco's founders, who were determined to base the company on the concept of open communication. Effective, sensitive feedback is an integral part of the culture. "We've created a living, breathing community where every employee has the right to give feedback on any topic," says Beau.

Cisco CEO John Chambers is famous for constantly articulating the Company's vision and values through staff sessions, chat sessions, all manager meetings, all employee meeting, and so forth. His constant themes are "open communication, teamwork and trust. It's the trust that's built into Cisco's culture that makes it possible for employees to talk about things that are unpleasant," according to Cisco's vice president of Human Resources, Barbara Beck.

Cisco's top management attributes much of its rapid growth to the lack of corporate militarism. Rather than seeking out people who will follow orders, they look for employees who will be self-motivated, who don't wait for people to tell them what to do. Cisco has rejected the notion that it is the manager's responsibility to give employees their objectives. Instead, Cisco believes in joint ownership, where the employee drafts his or her own goals and then reviews them with management. This allows employees to apply their own creativity towards achieving Cisco's corporate goals. As a result, Cisco has a very low turnover of employees, far smaller than that of Cabletron. By all accounts, Cisco, unlike Cabletron, is a fun place to work.

Two different companies—two different cultures—same target market. According to traditional business wisdom it would be hard-nosed Cabletron, not touchy-feeling Cisco that would win the war for market share. But that's not the case. Six years ago, Cabletron and arch-rival Cisco were booking about the same yearly revenue, about $180 million. By the beginning of

1997, Cisco was outselling Cabletron nearly 4 to 1. But what's even more telling is the difference between the productivity at the two companies. Each Cabletron employee generates about one-third as much revenue than each Cisco employee. Making work fun has allowed Cisco to earn multiple billions of dollars of extra.

Cisco's success relative to Cabletron offers ample evidence that it's counterproductive to treat people poorly. In fact, Cisco illustrates quite clearly that the best way to build revenue, productivity and market share is to create a work environment that values a sense of playfulness. That's the kind of environment that helps an organization build great relationships with partners, competitors and employees.

Case Study: The "De-Engineering" of Apple Computer

In the early 1980s, one of the exciting start-ups was Apple Computer. Founded by two young men in a California garage, Apple grew to be one of the most famous success stories of the computer industry. Co-founder and former president Steven Jobs believed that computing could become far simpler than it was at the time and he envisioned people being able to interact with computers as easily as they do with other common household appliances.

Job's vision became the Macintosh personal computer, a device that changed the way that we use computers. Although other fancy computers had preceded it, the Macintosh was the first inexpensive and practical computer to use a graphical user interface (GUI). The Macintosh GUI introduced the concept of icons. If you wanted to access a program, you pointed at an icon using a handheld mouse and clicked a button. This point-and-click interface, while common today, was virtually unknown outside research laboratories at that time.

When the Macintosh was launched, the most common personal computer was the IBM PC. The IBM PC ran an operating system called MS-DOS, a Microsoft product that required users to access programs by typing cryptic commands. Because the Macintosh was so much easier to use, Apple was able to charge a premium price for it, which made Apple among the most profitable companies in the computer industry.

However, Apple's ability to charge a premium price for the Macintosh was dependent on the clumsiness of MS-DOS. As soon as Microsoft's Windows version 3.0 hit the market in 1990, fewer users were willing to pay more for a Macintosh. Microsoft Windows, while not as easy to use as the Macintosh GUI, was still good enough to erode Apple's competitive advantage. Apple was forced to drop prices. Profit margins began to suffer and Apple's stock took a serious dip.

Apple could have stolen Microsoft's thunder if it had had the foresight to recode the Macintosh GUI so that it could run on the Intel-based IBM PC. This would have diminished the impact of Windows and likely would have propelled Apple into the highly favorable position that Microsoft enjoys today. True, in porting the Macintosh GUI, Apple would still have had to drop the price of the Macintosh hardware, but this would have become necessary in any case. Far better for Apple to lead the way than to be forced to react to Microsoft.

Why didn't Apple make this all-important move? To understand this, you need to understand Apple's corporate culture. Apple founder Steven Jobs was a management visionary. As the head of the Macintosh project, Steve installed in his employees an overwhelming desire to make the product successful. Long work hours were the norm. In 1983, the Macintosh development team wore T-shirts emblazoned with the motto: "Working 90 hours a week and loving every minute of it."

This enthusiasm had a downside as well. The long hours—once a matter of pride—had become an expectation; Apple became an unhealthy place in which to work. One rumor had it that certain managers had begun measuring productivity by the number of divorces in their group—the more divorces, the harder their people were working. Statistics bear this out: The divorce rate in Silicon Valley, where Apple was located, was "unsurpassed" according to Dennis Hayes, writing in the book *Behind the Silicon Curtain: The Seductions of Work in a Lonely Era* (South End Press, 1989). This kind of insensitivity to normal human needs had predictable consequences. By 1988, according to Hayes, an estimated 65 percent of Apple employees were "in therapy." The situation had gotten so bad that Apple was soliciting bids for an on-site psychotherapy facility.

While the company still employed many people who enjoyed their job, work there had lost the quality of playfulness. Some of this was the result of what I call the "de-engineering" of the company, as parts of Apple soon became infected with Industrial Age management ideas. Jobs was ousted from his leadership role. A palatial corporate headquarters was constructed, and senior executives were given big offices and even bigger perks. Former Microsoft executive vice president Mike Maples comments:

> For a number of years, Apple executives had automobiles bought by the company. They all traveled first class, and had limousines, and so forth. That extravagance became part of their culture and management felt entitled to such perks. At Microsoft, by contrast, everyone travels coach class, limousines are extremely uncommon, and everyone rents intermediate size cars or even uses taxicabs. Microsoft employees don't stay in the finest hotels, like Apple executives. But that's just part of our culture and what we think is the right thing to do.

As discussed earlier in this book, the problem with such perks is that they create a distance between managers and employees, making it seem like the top dogs are enjoying themselves at the expense of the workers. That's bad for morale and keeps people focused on "climbing the ladder" rather than enjoying their job. Predictably, Apple began catching other diseases of industrial age management as well. Jonathan Seybold explains:

> If you're looking for functional business models in the computer industry, do not look at Apple. It's remarkably dysfunctional, an environment where company politics has been raised to the level of art form.

In the face of this kind of behavior among its upper management, many Apple employees retreated into their work. The long hours and relentless self-sacrificing zealotry had turned many key Apple employees into exhausted, burned-out veterans. Under these circumstances, it's almost inevitable that Apple would stumble sooner or later. And stumble it did, at the worst time possible, just when the first real competition to its famous interface was about to be born.

Although many other factors contributed to Apple's ill-fated decision, the burnout of many Apple employees undoubtedly was a key problem. Employees who are burned out and unhealthy are likely to make poor decisions. Creativity dries up. The free flow of ideas—which is critical for success—becomes blocked. People running on automatic become irrational. Relationships break down inside the worker's family, between co-workers, customers, and suppliers.

Significantly, when Steven Jobs retook control of Apple in mid-1997, among the first things that he did was to vacate the palatial headquarters and eliminate the fancy offices that management had once taken for granted. As he told Time magazine, "This building has come to symbolize everything that went wrong with Apple. It's about corporate hubris. Greed."

A sense of fun and playfulness—something that's difficult when executives act like robber barons—is essential to success in today's market. In Silicon Valley culture, this sense of fun

TABLE 8.1
COMPARISON OF TOIL AND PLAY MINDSET

WORK = TOIL

- *Apathy.* People see work as an imposition in their lives, something to be gotten over with as soon as possible. Managers seek perks to make work more tolerable or so that they can lord it over the unfortunate peons beneath them.
- *Workaholism.* People get buried in emotionally dead, joyless work behaviors that seem productive but which are generally devoid of creativity and flexibility.
- *Burnout.* People become so tired and apathetic that decision making suffers. The organization loses all resilience and even positive change becomes impossible.

WORK = PLAY

- *Challenge.* People react positively to new ideas and new opportunities because they're seen as a way to enjoy the work experience more fully.
- *Energy.* Playful organizations have the extra energy to work the long hours that are sometimes necessary to get the job done.
- *Health.* The enjoyment of work removes much of the stress that creates poor health, creating a better quality of life.

comes from creating "insanely great products" (as Jobs puts it), not by awarding fancy management perks to the politically savvy. The difference between the two mindsets are shown in Table 8.1.

Business Strategies

Transforming work from toil into play may seem like a very difficult task. However, for the past five years I've asked hundreds of people: "What do you like most about your job." Somewhat to my surprise, the answer is almost always one of two responses: "I like the people," or "I like the challenge." I've also asked hundreds of people what they like least about their jobs. The most common answer: "I hate my boss." These two questions and answers, simple as they are, contain the secret to making working into something that people *want* to do. Transforming work into play simply requires that management tap into the natural desire of individuals to grow as individuals and to have good, friendly, relationships with their co-workers, suppliers, and customers. There are three keys to accomplishing this:

- *Cultivate constant challenge.*
- *Encourage informality.*
- *Create a sense of balance.*

STRATEGY 24: CULTIVATE CONSTANT CHALLENGE

The source of the employee's motivation makes a big difference in whether or not long work hours lead to burnout. Employees who work hard because they *want* to work hard are much less likely to burn out than employees who work hard because they *have* to work hard. Thus effective managers try to set up work situations where long hours aren't perceived as a burden because the work is interesting and challenging. Scott McNealy, CEO of Sun Microsystems, put it this way:

> *The only way you get burned out is when you have a frustrating or boring job. I know human nature well enough to know that if you give people fifty decks of cards all shuffled together and say, I want you to shuffle them, then sort them out into the proper decks in proper order, then reshuffle them, and do that again all day long, then you will have somebody burned out within four hours. But if you put them in a challenging job where they're learning along the way, driving new technologies and solving*

*interesting customer problems, they'll go home with a big smile
on their faces, feeling great about themselves, feeling great about
what they've done, feeling great about what they've learned. If
you have a fair, honest, diverse, equitable, challenging, exciting
work environment, there's nothing more you can do to pump
someone up. They just walk with a bounce in their step. I've
never felt bad about working somebody hard when we're working on fun stuff.*

Sally Narodick, former CEO of Edmark, agreed:

*We try to help people keep going until the product ships. It's a
very goal-driven organization but we try to be people-sensitive
and value people and their families. But the truth is that to work
in this business you need to be someone who has a passion about
making this happen and who wants to contribute entrepreneur-
ial drive to be able to survive here. We try to do it in a way that
lets people give a lot of what they have to give and really be valued. If you're using a good portion of your human potential and
if you're valued for your ideas, work is energizing, not draining.
That's what we try to do.*

In my many years of working with the Silicon Valley-style
companies, I've met an amazing number of employees who
were energized and jazzed by their jobs, more than in any
other industry. When I compare the attitude of an average Microsoft or Powersoft or Novell or Compaq employee with that
of the average worker on the street, I can't help but believe
that these companies are tapping into a powerful force leading
toward a healthier and more productive workplace.

This is not to say that every Silicon Valley employee is in love
with his or her job. People work long hours for different reasons. Some employees work long hours because they have a financial stake in the corporation. If the company does well, then
they'll be rewarded richly. Other employees work long hours

because they want to impress their peers. And some employees, even in the most enlightened organizations, sometimes work long hours merely because it's expected of them. However, the ideal inside the Silicon Valley business culture is to try to make every job as interesting and challenging and still avoid burnout.

STRATEGY 25: ENCOURAGE INFORMALITY

The traditional business world is an extremely formal place, with elaborate protocols for dress and behavior. These protocols were seen as a necessary means of maintaining control and order inside the corporation. When a worker dressed in a blue collar said "Yes, Sir" to a manager dressed in a suit, it was seen as a positive manifestation of "corporate respect." All was well in the world because the barriers separating management and workers were being strengthened.

By contrast, the entire thrust of the Silicon Valley management style is to remove the barriers between managers and workers, so that they all become peers. This makes it possible to have easier relationships between people in general—regardless of their function. To accomplish this, however, the formality that was such an important part of traditional business culture must be completely scrapped.

For the past 15 years, employees in companies with Silicon Valley cultures—management and staff alike—have rarely dressed in traditional business suits. Instead, business is comfortably carried on by people wearing T-shirts, sneakers, and blue jeans. This isn't to say that high-tech managers never wear suits. (In fact, when I interviewed Mitchell Kertzman, he was wearing an elegant business suit, albeit accessorized with red suspenders emblazoned with Mickey Mouse heads.) The point of not having a dress code isn't to replace one uniform with another. The idea is for people to dress however they feel is appropriate and however they feel comfortable. Wear a suit if you must, or dress down. It doesn't matter.

Dan Cerutti, a former IBM executive who started Massachusetts-based Amulet Software, explained:

> *What I wear is important. I go into work dressed casually because I find this to be an extremely beneficial aspect of the new culture. It's more comfortable, it's more informal. IBM and many other companies tend to be stuffy. I learned a long time ago that not wearing an expensive suit tells the engineers and the first-level people that you're just a normal person. When you dress like a normal person instead of some big business magnate, your employees see you as much more approachable.*

Casual dress echoes the casual way that people treat one another. Ceremony and ritual are replaced by comfortable interchanges that are much more productive than when communicating via a formal protocol. Michael Dell, CEO of Dell Computers, commented on the casual nature of the culture in his company:

> *It's open and not particularly formal in terms of orientation. I'd say it's much more of a meritocracy than at other companies. People don't go around calling each other "Mr." and "Ms." Everybody calls one another by his or her first name. You can show up for work in blue jeans if you want to. There are areas of the company where no one ever wears a tie. There are certainly no assigned parking spaces or executive anythings. It's basically an open, free-form culture where you can bump into everybody and talk. I get e-mail all the time form people everywhere in the company. And I always send them a message back.*

Other elements of informality, such as putting everyone on a first name basis, and eliminating management perks, also help create the informality that tends to make work more enjoyable. Some companies even dispense with job titles altogether, further breaking down the barriers between people inside the organization. The goal is to create an atmosphere where people feel comfortable, a workplace where they actually like to spend time. This, in turn, keeps people connected to the goals of the organization, which radically increases productivity.

STRATEGY 26: CREATE A
SENSE OF BALANCE

In a traditional business environment, one of the greatest challenges for managers is getting people to work harder for less money. To accomplish this, they institute rules and controls, motivate with threats, and so forth. These tactics often work—for a while—but they quickly alienate people, putting them at odds with the goals of the corporation. That's why unions are absolutely necessary inside traditional organizations—since the management has cast itself in the role of an oppressor, it's only fair that the workers can push back.

Unions, however, are exceedingly rare in Silicon Valley, primarily because they aren't seen as necessary by the workers themselves. This is because Silicon Valley companies have cultures that naturally treat workers well and which seek to make work into a positive experience. In fact, when the principles in this book are consistently applied, employees can become so motivated that they actually can work too hard—of their own volition.

I heard a story recently about a company that makes software for the Internet. I'm not certain if the story is true, but it does illustrate how utterly different Silicon Valley companies are from the rest of the business world. According to the story, the CEO thought that the company's employees needed a day off, so he told them *not* to come in on the upcoming weekend. Many employees came into work anyway. On the next weekend, the parking lot of the facility had been blocked off with orange parking cones, effectively preventing employees from coming into work on the weekend.

This is not the kind of problem that comes up inside traditional corporations.

Wise managers realize that nothing kills fun more than making it into an obsession. That's why they encourage employees to have a sense of balance in their lives. Silicon Valley managers want employees to enjoy their jobs, but not the exclusion of everything else in their lives. Michael Dell, CEO of Dell Computer, explained:

> This is a very challenging business that continues to present me and everyone that's involved in it with opportunities to learn and grow. We're always doing something that's very exciting and new, whether it's expanding in Asia or launching into a new product segment. However, there's a limit to the number of productive hours a person can actually work. There's also only so much fun you can have before it starts to be not as much fun.

Thus, effective high-tech managers try to encourage a sense of balance inside their organizations. Mitchell Kertzman, CEO of Sybase, commented:

> My philosophy is that you've got to have balance between your work life and your personal life. I want people to work very hard when they're here, and they do. But I want them to be as happy at home as at work, and to be as giving to their families as they are to Powersoft. In the long run, that creates the best work environment. Happy people do the best work. Balanced people do the best work. So, it's very important to me that people have that balance.

Because long working hours are sometimes going to be the rule, many people inside high-tech organizations make it a habit to disconnect from work on a regular basis. Some simply won't take work home with them. They leave their home life as a haven away from work, turning the abbreviated time with their families into "quality" time. Jim Manzi, former CEO of Lotus, commented on how he does this in his own life.

I come to work very early in the morning, and, if I'm not travel-ing, I go home for dinner, and I don't bring work home. It's as simple as that. I can't work any harder than I do, and if I tried, I would just be pretending. I spend an enormous amount of time and energy on this place but there are limits. I communicate it openly in the company that everybody has to find their own bal-ance. It's an individual decision about how you want to be in your own life and how you want to balance yourself. It's not some law that I will dictate. I believe in individuals making their own decisions about what's important in their lives and finding their own point of balance and making those trade-offs.

Ann Palermo, former vice president of worldwide market-ing for the PCDOCS document management software com-pany (and a mother of two), takes a similar approach:

I don't talk about work at all when I'm at home. I've learned to pick up at 5:30 and leave the office. You have to be able to accept that work will never be finished. Nothing is ever "done." Some people think of it as a treadmill, but I know that even if I spend three times as much time at the office, there would still be more to do. You can't be home on the weekend thinking "I'll never get this project done." You just have to be able to leave it alone. It's a men-tal discipline, I suppose, although some people might say that I'm in denial. I don't know how people survive without being able to set it aside.

For the people who practice this strategy, keeping their home life sacred helps create a sense of balance and perspective. By setting aside their work for a while, they find it easier to be productive when they return to their demanding schedules.

Employees in Silicon Valley-style organizations also develop hobbies and interests that help them forget work for a while. Former Microsoft executive vice president Mike Maples described how he sees the employees at Microsoft:

> *One of the things that's really hard to represent about Microsoft is the dimensions of the characters and the interests that the people have. Most books make its characters pretty unidimensional. But, like any place, the people at Microsoft have a lot of dimensions. There are a lot of musicians around, people with weird hobbies, virtually anything you can think of. The trade-off that people make at a Microsoft is that they have three or four passions rather than a dozen passions that are important to them in life. Whether those passions are family, or church, or activities, or hobbies, or mountain climbing or whatever, almost everybody at Microsoft has a number of things that interest them beside Microsoft. However, the number of those things is probably less than at other companies.*

The key is make certain that you have some way to temporarily disconnect with the demanding ebb and flow of work. Industry guru Jonathan Seybold explained how he achieves this balance:

> *You've got to moderate yourself. There are times when I very deliberately do not read my electronic mail or answer my voice mail. There are other time when we have something important taking place, where I will check in during the weekend several times. When there's breaking news, you want to tune in and find out what's happening. In the same way, if there's a decision to make, we can get a lot done between Friday night and Monday morning. However, you only want to do that when there's something going on that makes it worthwhile. If you get in a habit of*

SUCCESS SECRETS FROM SILICON VALLEY

*doing it all the time, you'll never have good decisions. You end up
spending more of your time cleaning up messes and having less
of your resources available to really get things done.*

Work at Silicon Valley-style companies often has seasonal
rhythms based on whether a new product is under development, or there is a spate of trade shows to attend, and so
forth. One way to achieve balance is to match the rhythms of
life to the rhythms of work. Carol Bartz, CEO of AutoDesk,
commented on this challenge:

> *People spend too much of their time trying to be the perfect exec-
> utive, or the perfect technologist, the perfect mom or dad, the per-
> fect partner, the perfect corporate citizen or social citizen, and so
> forth. If you try to pull off all that stuff every day or every week,
> you will burn out. There's no doubt about it. There are times, for
> example, when you've got a product to release, when you've got
> to say to your family, "I'll see you in a month." There are other
> times when you've got to say to the company, "I've got a new
> baby, or my daughter's having her birthday party and I'll see
> you next week." You have to figure out how to change your prior-
> ities and not make everything be as important as everything else
> all the time. It doesn't mean that home is more important than
> work or work more important than home. It just means that you
> have to take each of them singularly.*

Truly effective leaders promote a better sense of balance by
giving employees a certain amount of flexibility about coming
into work, especially when things are slow. Bill Gross, CEO of
Knowledge Adventure explained:

> *I'm definitely concerned about people becoming burned out. We
> have been able to manage that by still giving people complemen-
> tary time off when they finish a crunch project. We also try to*

stagger the cycles of the crunches so that people can rejuvenate. When people are simply too exhausted to do their work here, mobile computing allows them to work from Lake Tahoe or from home for a few days to recuperate but still stay in touch without delaying a project.

Some companies even sanction sabbaticals that give employees the opportunity to collect their thoughts and reestablish balance in their lives. Carol Bartz, CEO of AutoDesk, told about the program in her company:

After four years, people get a six-week sabbatical, which they often combine with their vacation to take eight or ten weeks off. That can be very controversial, and I've heard other companies say that people don't come back and so forth. However, I think that a sabbatical really does revive people. It gives them a chance to get away for a couple of months, get a perspective on things, travel around the world, spend time with their families, live with a newborn, whatever, and people tend to come back really energized. I make a strong statement in a lot of my speeches about balance.

How Evolved Is Your Organization?

The following quiz assesses your organization's ability to transform work from a necessary evil into a positive aspect of life:

••

The Following Is True . . .

	Always	Frequently	Sometimes	Seldom	Never
1. The work around here is often boring.	____	____	____	____	____
2. We're strictly on a first-name basis.	____	____	____	____	____
3. There are rules against decorating your work area.	____	____	____	____	____
4. Sometimes we all take off together for a sporting event.	____	____	____	____	____
5. Loud laughter would sound out-of-place here.	____	____	____	____	____
6. I'd rather be at work than doing a hobby.	____	____	____	____	____
7. Our top managers generally look like they're constipated.	____	____	____	____	____
8. Nothing is so serious here that we can't laugh about it.	____	____	____	____	____
9. The management gets angry if people post Dilbert cartoons.	____	____	____	____	____
10. Our managers don't press people to work unpaid overtime.	____	____	____	____	____

••

Scoring:

For all odd-numbered statements, score:

Always	1
Frequently	2
Sometimes	3
Seldom	4
Never	5

For all even-numbered statements, score:

Always	5
Frequently	4
Sometimes	3
Seldom	2
Never	1

If your score is 10–20: Your organization is a difficult and unhappy place in which to work. There's an overwhelming feeling of negativity that affects everyone's attitude. You'd probably rather be anyplace else than at work.

If your score is 21–35: Your organization is average. You share the good times, you share the bad times. There are days when you think that you enjoy your job, but most of the time it's pretty much of a drag. You often wonder if it's better anywhere else.

If your score is 36–50: Your organization is close to the Silicon Valley ideal. People really enjoy their jobs and are more than willing to spend extra time at work. It's common to hear laughter in the hallways. It's a fun place and you wonder how people exist in the depressing world of traditional business culture.

Points to Ponder

In order to create leverage for change, write out the answers to the following questions:

- How much less stress would you feel if you really enjoyed your job? Do you think that this would make you more healthy? Do you think that you would live longer?

  _____

  _____

  _____

  _____

- Every day you're influencing the quality of your work environment and that of the people around you. What could you do tomorrow in order to make work a more pleasurable experience?

  _____

  _____

  _____

  _____

- Do the people around you think that work is a hassle or something that can make their lives richer and more exciting? What kind of people would make your team into a joyful powerhouse?

  _____

  _____

  _____

  _____

- When was the last time that you told somebody "I really love my job!" What were you feeling when you said it? How can you recapture that feeling?

  _____

  _____

  _____

  _____

My Challenge to You

By the end of our lives, we will have spent approximately a quarter of our waking hours at work, more time than we're likely to spend doing anything else. Do we really want to spend this precious time working at jobs we don't enjoy, with peers we don't trust, for bosses we secretly despise?

Where I go, I meet people who are deeply dissatisfied with their jobs, who feel underutilized yet overworked, patronized and pandered to, apathetic and unmotivated. I see middle managers who are lonely, unhappy, and paranoid, who hate their jobs yet are terrified of losing them. I watch executives who, despite their high salaries, are dazed and confused, following business strategies that have long since lost their meaning and effectiveness. How sad and yet how unnecessary!

A business culture is reestablished every day when people go to work under the same mindsets. Most don't realize—or believe—they are free to choose new ways of doing business that will lead toward greater success in the future. So why don't more companies make the transition to a more powerful and flexible culture? Why do they wait until the market forces change upon them?

Traditional business culture often results in a situation in which the mindsets must change before the mindsets can change. People who have internalized the old culture have deep-seated beliefs that change is dangerous, complicated, and painful. They can't believe that everything could change immediately, if the people within the culture simply decided to adopt, and act on, a new set of beliefs.

It is that simple. The process of cultural transformation is nothing more than a series of personal decisions, made by people throughout an organization, to think about problems in new ways. If even one person has the courage to laugh out loud at a pompous presentation, or the wisdom to treat fellow workers as respected peers, an organization becomes more healthy. The challenge is one of leadership, not just at the top of the organization, but everywhere people interact and work together. It requires that people make a choice, a decision about what they really want.

That decision may require leaving your current position and finding employment in an organization that's better adapted to the Information Age and your way of thinking. But if you remain where you are, it's your responsibility and obligation to use the knowledge you've obtained and whatever leadership ability you possess to help create a workplace that's productive, humane, and fun.

A phrase that you hear a lot inside Silicon Valley companies is "we're going to change the world." We all realize that technology is making an incredible impact on every aspect of our daily lives and that the pace of innovation moving faster every year as raw computer power becomes ever less expensive. However, it's culture, not technology, that determines how effectively that technology is used.

Technology is an enabler rather than a driver of cultural change. It's regrettable that so much attention is given to the products of Silicon Valley and so little to the unique cultures that has come from the new culture. This book, I hope, begins to remedy this oversight. A hundred years from now, Bill Gates and his colleagues will be history, and today's computers will be gathering dust in museums. In the long run, the legacy of Silicon Valley may not be their technology, but this new corporate culture. Perhaps that's what really meant when high-tech leaders say "we're going to change the world."

Be part of the transformation!

Appendix A

....

EIGHT KEYS TO A
SILICON VALLEY CULTURE

....

Key No. 1:
Business Is an Ecosystem, Not a Battlefield

Conventional wisdom says business is a series of conflicts between companies, departments, groups, and individuals. As a result, managers build big empires, full of "troops" that won't and can't do anything without orders from the boss. In Silicon Valley culture, Business is treated as an Ecosystem consisting of symbiotic relationships formed to exploit market niches, and the company that is the most diverse is the most likely to thrive. As a result, companies always adapt quickly to new market conditions.

Key No. 2:
Corporations Are Communities, Not Machines

Conventional wisdom says that an organization is a system in which employees are faceless, replaceable cogs. As a result, managers create rigid "systems" with rigid roles and responsibilities, centralizing control at the top. In Silicon Valley culture, an organization is a community whose purpose is to realize the hopes and dreams of the individuals inside it. As a result, employees are dedicated to the organization's goals and enjoy contributing to its success.

Key No. 3:
Management Is Service, Not Control

Conventional wisdom says that the manager's job is to command and control employee behavior. As a result, management becomes micromanagement while individual initiative is killed in favor of a "let's wait and see what the boss says" mentality. In Silicon Valley culture, management is seen as a service role. Managers set directions and to obtain the resources that employees need to get the job done. As a result, teams form their own rules and accomplish tasks without the overhead of bureaucracy.

Key No. 4:
Employees Are Peers, Not Children

Conventional wisdom says that most employees are too immature and foolish to be assigned real authority. As a result, employees only work when they're being watched, if then, often spending more time "covering their butts" than doing productive work. In Silicon Valley culture, employees are considered the peers of managers. Excellence is expected and encouraged everywhere from the loading dock to the boardroom. As a result, employees at all levels take charge of their own destinies and their contribution to the whole.

Key No. 5:
Motivate with Vision, Not Fear

Conventional wisdom says that employees only work because they're afraid of getting fired. As a result, work becomes a loathsome experience filled with truckling, ass-kissing, and compulsive corporate politicking. In Silicon Valley culture, companies seek a compelling vision that drives away fear. People know where they're going and are amply rewarded when they get there. As a result, employees work hard, not out of fear, but because they believe in the organization's goals.

Key No. 6:
Change Is Growth, Not Pain

Conventional wisdom says that change is complicated and difficult, something that companies only undergo if they're in desperate shape. As a result, change efforts fail as people in the organization torpedo and sabotage what they're afraid will be painful. In Silicon Valley culture, change is a desirable process of adapting to new market conditions. As a result, employees embrace new ideas, new ways of doing business, and new ways of making profit.

Key No. 7:
Computers Are Servants, Not Masters

Conventional wisdom says that the primary role of technology is to strengthen management's command and control over the rest of the company. As a result, employees become dehumanized and demoralized, mere attachments to the computer. In Silicon Valley culture, computers are seen as valuable servants that eliminate repetitive and boring work, thus freeing human beings to be creative and to build better business relationships. As a result, organizations learn faster and coordinate activities more effectively.

Appendix B

Key No. 8:
Transform Work into Play, Not Toil

Conventional wisdom says that work is a necessary evil that takes time away from the things that one would rather be doing. As a result, people resent going to work, creating endless conflict, passive aggression and endless stress. In Silicon Valley culture, people believe that work is something that is supposed to be enjoyable. The job of management is to help put people in jobs that will truly satisfy them. As a result, employees actually want to spend more time at the workplace.

Strategy 8: Encourage Creative Dissent

The combination of diversity of opinion and dispersion of power naturally creates an atmosphere where people disagree on the approaches to be taken. Make this dissent, and the resolution that inevitably follows, part of the process of creating new value.

Strategy 9: Build Autonomous Teams

Rather than organizing along broad functional lines, make certain that each product and service has a team that's dedicated to the success of that product and service. Make certain that the team actually has the decision-making power to get things done.

Strategy 10: Hire the Self-Motivated

When hiring and promoting, locate or cultivate people who don't require direction and who aren't spoiled by Industrial Age habits. This will help influence everybody else in the organization to act in a more independent fashion.

Strategy 11: Eliminate Fancy Perks

Avoid the kind of perks that create distance between managers and employees. Integrate the management and executive staff into the base of employees so that everyone feels as if they are part of the same community.

Strategy 12:
Sacrifice the Sacred Cows

Craft dramatic opportunities to separate people from the old ways and simultaneously create a strong emotional linkage to a more positive culture.

Strategy 13: *Create a Climate of Trust*

Look for opportunities to build trust between individuals, teams, and organizations. Always act in a way that's congruent with a personal sense of honesty and honor.

Strategy 14: *Build a Shared Vision*

Make certain that there is a shared vision that resonates with everybody in the organization. Make sure that, within the context of that vision, everybody knows what mission they're supposed to be accomplishing.

Strategy 15:
Compensate for Missions Accomplished

Tie extra, team-based compensation to the accomplishment of the mission at hand, within the larger context of the corporate vision. Make certain that the success of the organization translates into the success of the individuals it includes.

Strategy 16: *Ruthlessly Prioritize*

Don't let the increased flow of information create a state of overflow. Understand where you're going and make certain that you're surrounded by information that helps you achieve that goal.

Strategy 17:
Have Long-Term Vision, Short-Term Plans

Look ahead to the future for guidance, but don't waste time mapping out a detailed plan to get there. Instead, concentrate on what needs to be done next to move you closer to your ultimate goal.

Strategy 18:
Keep Jobs Fluid and Flexible

Don't bother writing detailed job descriptions and trying to set up a "system." Instead, let individuals, teams, and organizations define themselves as necessary to accomplish the job at hand.

Strategy 19:
Make Decisions Quickly and Broadly

Promote an environment where important decisions receive lively debate from all levels of the organization. Then drive the decision to a close.

Strategy 20:
Hope for the Best, Prepare for the Worst

Make certain that everyone knows that layoffs are a fact of life. Encourage individuals and organizations to have contingency plans in case worse comes to worst.

Strategy 21:
Use Electronic Mail to Flatten Management

Use electronic mail to eliminate layers of management approval and to keep people in remote locations connected to the goals and social fabric of the corporate community.

Strategy 22:
Humanize Electronic Communications

Don't use electronic mail to avoid difficult communications. Use personal contact and telephone contact to build better business relationships.

Strategy 23: Reduce Information Pollution

Be certain that your personal use of electronic mail doesn't create new communications problems in the organization. Write like a journalist so that people can absorb and understand your ideas as quickly and easily as possible.

Strategy 24: Cultivate Constant Challenge

Avoid burnout by making certain that your job and the jobs of your employees are interesting and exciting.

Strategy 25: Encourage Informality

Put everybody on a first-name basis and let every day be "casual day." Create an environment where people feel as if they're at home with their friends and family.

Strategy 26:
Create a Sense of Balance

Find a physical or mental space where you can escape from the daily demands of the work environment. Learn to set complicated tasks aside when you need to rest. Take time off to "recharge your batteries."

Index

Index

Index

Index

Index

Index

Index